FROM
GENERATION
TO
GENERATION

FROM GENERATION TO GENERATION

THE STORY OF
YOUTH IN THE
WORLD COUNCIL
OF CHURCHES

ANS J. VAN DER BENT

World Council of Churches, Geneva

Cover design: Michael Dominguez/WCC

Cover photos: WCC, John Taylor, Peter Müller, Nair Benedicto

ISBN 2-8254-0844-1

Printed in Switzerland

To

PHILIP A. POTTER

Contents

Introduction

This book about youth in the ecumenical movement from 1925 onwards, and youth in the World Council of Churches from its inception in 1948, is dedicated to Philip A. Potter. He has made more contributions to youth work than anybody else in the Council. Philip Potter joined the staff of the Youth Department in 1954, and was its director from 1957 to 1960. He was the chairman of the World Student Christian Federation from 1960 to 1968, director of World Mission and Evangelism from 1967 to 1972, and general secretary of the World Council of Churches from 1972 to 1984.

The book draws on the extensive archives on youth in the library of the Ecumenical Centre in Geneva. The chapters were shared with persons who were deeply involved in the ecumenical life and the activities of the young people at one stage or another. I am indebted to all of them for their valuable comments and criticism.

The list of conferences and consultations and a bibliography of official ecumenical literature on Christian youth included in the book will help the reader to gain a more systematic knowledge of youth activities in the ecumenical movement.

Youth work in the World Council of Churches has focused on the age range of 18-25, or 18-30. In North America, "youth" has normally meant the 13-18 age range, sometimes the 16-18 high school range. At one time there was an agreement that the World Council of Christian Education would deal with youth under 18, and the World Council of Churches with those over 18. This explains the character of the many different programmes and activities of the Council's Youth Department.

The book starts with ecumenical youth work from the year 1925. It should be remembered, however, that international Christian youth work had already begun in the previous century. The chief ecumenical agencies were the YMCA, the YWCA, and the Student Christian Movement (SCM). The World Alliance of YMCAs was founded in 1844, the World

YWCA in 1855. Their objectives in those early years were essentially evangelistic and missionary; their constant endeavour to fulfill these aims made them the pioneers of ecumenism. As they were not unduly concerned over the relations with the churches until the 1920s, both organizations were able to develop from Protestant origins into fully interconfessional bodies, and included in their programmes Orthodox and Roman Catholic youth, and even young people of other faiths.

The Student Christian Movements, also evangelical in nature, were on the other hand from the beginning conscious of the vital importance of their relations with the churches, and at an early period took up the cause of Christian unity. They were led by students on behalf of students. As they were movements rather than organizations, they enjoyed a certain freedom denied to institutionalized agencies. The World Student Christian Federation was founded in 1895 through the vision and drive of John R. Mott, expressing the universality of the SCMs in many nations. It helped generations of students to understand and experience a quality of Christian discipleship and to grow in a profound awareness of the oikoumene in Christ.

The biography of John R. Mott by C. Howard Hopkins, published by the World Council of Churches in 1979, describes the decisive influence of this ecumenical pioneer on the international youth movements and refers to the key role the WSCF played in the middle of this century. Many leaders of national SCMs became prominent leaders in the WCC. *The Student World*, published by the WSCF from 1908-69, was a major journal mediating ecumenical vision to generations of young people.

When the Second World War broke out, the leaders of the three youth movements, together with the Provisional Committee of the World Council of Churches, established an informal emergency committee of Christian organizations, which paved the way for more official cooperation among the four bodies after the war.

I regret that the World Alliance of YMCAs, the World YWCA and the WSCF have not received greater attention in this book. Although the ecumenical relations between these three bodies and the World Council of Churches have been fruitful in many respects, the scope of this book does not provide for a more detailed treatment. An effort should be made in the future to tell the story of their inter-relatedness and their joint efforts in many fields. There are earlier histories of the YMCA, the YWCA and the WSCF, but all of them need updating.

The German theologian Dietrich Bonhoeffer played an important role in the ecumenical youth movement in the thirties. At the dramatic conference of the Universal Christian Council for Life and Work in Fanø,

Denmark, in 1934, he led the German youth delegation. It was probably at Berlin during August of the same year that Bonhoeffer drafted eight theses concerning youth work in the church. He said that "the future of the church does not depend on youth but only on Jesus Christ. The task of young people is not reorganization of the church but listening to God's Word; the church's task is not the conquest of young people, but the teaching of the Gospel."

Bonhoeffer strongly expressed his conviction that the problem of communication between successive generations does not exist; young people have no special status or privilege within the Christian community. "They should serve the community by listening to the Gospel, by learning it and practising it." In his last thesis he strongly emphasized that only the church counts, not any church organization or Christian club, including Christian youth organs. "Every church institution discredits the being of the church. They must be regarded as makeshifts and have therefore only relative importance."[1]

This view was shared by Albert H. van den Heuvel, executive secretary of the WCC Youth Department from 1964 to 1968. Included in an excellent collection of essays on Christian youth published in 1965 is a short and critical history of youth work in which he concludes that "youth work is allowed only because of the hardness of our hearts; it must be seen under the aspect of God's patience rather than God's will. Youth work in the church is an anomaly, like denominations and rummage sales. They may be allowed, but they are not self-evident... Where the *ekklesia* is discovered, the generations are united."[2]

Throughout this book we emphasize that young people *are* the church *now* in their sector of the world's life. Youth growing in its own cultural environment represents the ceaseless process by which the body of Christ takes form in the midst of an evolving world. The freedom of young people to testify to God's freedom determines the shape of their witness.

It is hoped that the following pages will illustrate the dialectical and dynamic process of God's dealing with the generations in the middle and latter part of this century. It is a story of deep involvement in healing the divisions of the world, of the common joy of the forgiveness of sins, of both old and young people, and of their celebrations of salvation.

NOTES

[1] *Gesammelte Schriften*, Band III, Munich, Chr. Kaiser Verlag, 1960, pp.292-93.
[2] "A Short and Critical History of Youth", in *The New Creation and the New Generation*, New York, Friendship Press, 1965, pp.75 and 79.

I. The Ecumenical Youth Commission, 1933-39

"We turn to the young of all countries. With keen appreciation we have heard of their aspirations and efforts for a better social order as expressed in the youth movements of many lands. We desire to enlist the ardour and energy of youth, the freshness and fullness of their life, in the service of the kingdom of God and humanity."[1]

That was part of the message of the First Universal Christian Conference on Life and Work which took place in Stockholm in 1925. The message contained five affirmations: (1) that the call of the hour to the church is a call to repentance; (2) that the churches should accept the urgent duty of applying the gospel of Christ in all realms of life — political, international and industrial; (3) that shared faith leads to the experience of the unity of the church of Christ; (4) that the church is by its nature universal; and (5) that in the crucified and risen Lord alone lies the hope of the world.

The Stockholm conference was the first major attempt to get separated and isolated churches of many countries to collaborate on common tasks. The large international gathering, under the chairmanship of Archbishop Nathan Söderblom, was a landmark in the recognition by the churches of their social responsibility. Stockholm, like the World Missionary Conference at Edinburgh in 1910, set up a Continuation Committee which, five years later, gave place to a more permanent organization called the Universal Christian Council for Life and Work. The declared objective of the Council was "to perpetuate and strengthen the fellowship between the churches in the application of Christian ethics to the social problems of modern life".[2]

"Youth today is really in an unenviable situation. It is conscious of the epic of the days of the Great War and realizes that it lives in days of an aftermath. It wants something big to challenge it to be as great as the youth of two decades ago. Youth knows that there should be such a challenge but that it should not lead to war."[3] So said J.C. Bacon in a pamphlet in 1931 when he introduced the World Alliance for Promoting International Friendship through the Churches and its concern for youth. The World Alliance was founded at Constance, Germany, in 1914. It maintained a close relationship with the Church Peace Union. The Alliance was chiefly the outcome of the vision and devotion of an English layman, Lord Willoughby Dickinson, and it was strongly supported by many church leaders in Europe and America.

The Alliance called an international conference at the Hague in 1919. Its Declaration of Principles said: "We therefore are convinced that the time has come when a strenuous effort should be made by all Christians to realize all that is implied in Christ's teaching of the brotherhood of mankind, and to impress alike upon themselves and upon others that here alone lies the hope of permanent peace among the nations, and of any true solution of social and industrial problems."[4] Faithful to its purpose to help substitute reason and arbitration for war as a means of settling international disputes, the Alliance discussed disarmament at several of its conferences.

There were at the Conference at Prague in 1928 some twenty German students who had obtained special permission to attend. The conference passed a resolution calling upon the national councils of the Alliance to give greater attention to work among youth. Two international youth conferences were held in the following year, one in cooperation with the *Chevaliers de la Paix* at Vaumarcus and the other at Westerburg. But both these gatherings were dominated by older people.

At the eighth international conference of the World Alliance for International Friendship through the Churches (Cambridge, 1931) the delegations from each of the thirty-three national councils included younger members who were youth leaders in their churches. These younger delegates met on their own a few days before the conference and considered ways in which church youth organizations could play an effective role in promoting mutual understanding between the churches and among the nations of the world. The youth delegates asked the Council of the Alliance "to proceed with the work which has been begun: (a) by giving the Youth Commission a more complete organization; (b) by increasing the opportunities for contact between young people, in the form of conferences or travel; (c) by recommending to the national councils that they should give youth a place in their midst".[5]

According to the minutes of the first meeting of the Youth Commission of the World Alliance held in London, 4 April 1932, three youth secretaries were appointed: Dr Dietrich Bonhoeffer (Germany), Rev.

P.C. Toureille (France) and Rev. F.W.T. Craske (Great Britain). The secretaries would be in correspondence with the national councils in their respective countries. The Management Committee of the Alliance had voted SFr. 6000 for the work of the Youth Commission. Plans were made for a first youth study conference, to be held at Gland, Switzerland, 24-31 August 1932.

At its very first session in August 1925, the Continuation Committee of Life and Work appointed a commission to ensure cooperation with young people. In conjunction with the other Christian world youth organizations located in Geneva, it arranged from 1930-32 three series of lively study weeks, which showed a refreshing disregard for ecclesiastical prudence. The study weeks dealt with problems of industrial relations, the world's economic interdependence, unemployment, the maladjustment of production and consumption, and international efforts towards social peace.

The objectives as well as the constituencies of the Universal Christian Council for Life and Work and the World Alliance for International Friendship through the Churches were the same at many points. Much of their work was jointly carried out. In fact in certain countries they were organically one body. This led to the merger of some of their departments on an international basis as well and, in April 1933, in response to a widely felt need, a joint Ecumenical Youth Commission was formed at a meeting held at Luneray (Seine inférieure), France. It was not an independent body, only a group "commissioned" by its two parent bodies, officially answerable to and supported by their constituent church bodies, which represented a number of non-Roman Catholic churches.

The Ecumenical Youth Commission sponsored annual international and regional conferences for Christian youth leaders, coordinated the selection and preparation of a group of younger leaders to take part in the Second World Conference on Church and Society in Oxford in 1937, and planned for the First World Conference of Christian Youth in Amsterdam in 1939. It dealt directly with representative national youth liaison groups in many countries as well as with youth departments of individual churches in other nations. It consisted of 11 members and 22 corresponding members, representing a great variety of churches and the principal youth movements. Henry-Louis Henriod (France), joint general secretary of the World Alliance and Life and Work from 1933 onwards, functioned as its chairman and Th. de Félice (Switzerland) as its secretary, replaced in 1936 by R.H. Edwin Espy (United States).

Youth and the Church, published probably in 1929, is a mine of information on conditions and currents in the life of youth in the twenties and early thirties. It was a report to the Continuation Committee of the

Stockholm Conference on Life and Work by its Youth Commission. Basil Mathews, one of the editors of the book, depicts vividly the socio-political upheavals of the time and their profound impact on youth. According to him, problems of youth are centred in four areas of life: "The home, and in particular sex problems; patriotism, and in particular the individual facing military service; thirdly, inter-racial and international friction; and fourthly, lifework in a mechanized, impersonal, industrial civilization."[6]

In his contribution on "The Church and Educated Youth", W.A. Visser 't Hooft, from 1924-31 secretary of the World Committee of Young Men's Christian Associations, dwells at length on modern secondary education, moral relativism, youth in search of reality, and the direct educational activities of the church. He notes that modern education has become a force which now shapes the life of nations as a whole, and it undermines traditional social, racial and family values. Unfortunately science is taught in schools as if it had all the ultimate answers to the problems of life. Youth is much less eager to take up the study of history, philosophy, art and literature.

In many societies general moral standards are breaking down. Family life is disintegrating. Youth is not being led in helpful ways in its search for an ethics of life. "Is there not rather decadence and retrogression, if it is true that in one of the most cultural nations of Europe doctors assert that sexual relationships and diseases are wide-spread among the pupils of the higher classes of our secondary schools?" Visser 't Hooft asks.[7]

The question of the relationship of religion to the curriculum of schools needs to be newly examined. Large sections of secondary school youth must recover contact with Christianity, either through private Christian schools, religious instruction in public schools, direct educational activities of the church such as Sunday school and catechism, or through voluntary Christian movements working among young people. "If Christianity would show itself once more an aggressive and effective factor in the shaping of human society, youth would need less convincing as to its justification for existence."[8]

The other contributions to *Youth and the Church* also express the conviction that the role of youth is crucial for human progress. They underline the urgency to challenge young people to face the claims of the kingdom.

The various conferences organized or sponsored by the Ecumenical Youth Commission of the World Alliance and Life and Work (its offices were located in 2 rue de Montchoisy, Geneva) reflect a wide range of concerns, aims and activities. The main issues considered at a conference in Gland, Switzerland, 24-31 August 1932, were: (1) the message of the church in the present crisis; (2) the meaning of the kingdom of God; (3) the question of the social environment of the church, especially (a) nationalism; (b) injustice in international relations; (c) modern collectivism; (d) the necessity for international planning; (e) unemployment and immediate relief; (f) the menace of the "machine"; (g) disarmament; (h) revision of treaties.

Concentrating on the questions of the will of God for our present situation and the meaning of the kingdom of God, the English discussion group, chaired by F.W.T. Craske, identified three forms of the kingdom: in the person of Jesus Christ, in the ongoing struggle between Christ and anti-Christ, and its perfect manifestation in God's own time. In the German group, presided by Dietrich Bonhoeffer, there was no agreement as to whether the will of God manifests itself in the individual soul or in the church which must witness to it through its judgment of capitalism and nationalism.

Another international youth conference was held again at Gland, 29 August-4 September 1933. This time the theme was "The Task of the Church in the Social International Crisis". Presentations were made on "The Christian Philosophy and the Individual", "The Christian Philosophy and the State", "The Christian Philosophy and the World Community", and "The Christ and the New Humanity".

Members of the fifth International Conference of Youth meeting at Fanø, 22-29 August 1934, studied the theme "Churches and Christians and the Problem of the State". Resolutions were passed on conscientious objection and on the universal nature of the church. The first resolution expressed the opinion that "the rights of conscience, undertaken in obedience to God's Word, exceed in importance those of any state whatever" and was carried unanimously. The second resolution said that "the church has for its essential task the preaching of the Word of God. Therefore, it could not be a function (even the highest function) of the nation. The church works within the nation, but it is not 'of the nation'... the church, although it should not enter political struggles, ought, however, to urge its members to study social and political questions, with a view to action. This action, for which they are responsible individually, should have as its result the building up of a state where there is entire freedom for the Christian life." Both resolutions were presented to the meeting of the Universal Christian Council for Life and Work at Fanø on 28 August 1934.

The influence of Dietrich Bonhoeffer on the meeting was considerable. Before his arrival he had insisted that the German youth sector should uncompromisingly uphold the Barmen declaration of heresy which was issued in the same year on 31 May. In a letter to Th. de Félice he had written that the members of his delegation would not attend if representatives of the German church government were to be present. Consequently the German delegation consisted almost solely of Bonhoeffer's former students in Berlin. It was Bonhoeffer in particular who emphasized the universal (anti-nationalist) nature of the church and the superiority of God's commandments over all claims of the state. He also insisted that the words "any war whatsoever", instead of "aggressive war", should be retained.

A memorandum from the Youth Committee of the British Council of the World Alliance was submitted at Fanø requesting official representation for this committee on the International Youth Commission. From October 1934 to February 1936 three issues of the *Fanø Fellowship* in English, French and German were circulated among the delegates of the Fanø Youth Conference.

The International Youth Conference at Chamby, Montreux, 2 to 8 August 1935, focused on the theme of "Liberty and Authority". At the youth conference in La Borcaderie, Neuchatel, 8-14 September 1936, more delegates from Africa and Asia were present than at previous meetings. The theme was "Christian Youth and the Way to Peace". Most participants shared the view that "the use of arms cannot promote international justice in any circumstance, because violence releases the elements of hatred, which is not conducive to an abiding peace". There was a considerable divergence of opinion on the question as to whether "the churches would be justified in asking for an international force to maintain and safeguard order". There was general agreement that "the pacifists would today render a better service to humanity as a whole if they would concentrate on striving for a better social and international order instead of formulating what steps ideal pacifists must take in case of an outbreak of war".

The conference of the Ecumenical Youth Commission at Budapest, 13-16 November 1936, was concerned with the strengthening of national relations. Reports from countries like Bulgaria, Czechoslovakia, Poland, Austria, Yugoslavia and Hungary revealed that each nation faced different hopes and problems. There was need to work towards supportive solidarity. In the report of the conference, edited by André Bouvier, it was stressed that "the biblical foundations of ecumenism are the messianic vision of the prophets, the coming of the Messiah, the unity of the human race, the announcement of the Suffering Servant, the realization and incarnation in Christ, his teaching both individual and social, his message of the kingdom, both present and future".

One hundred youth visitors sat in the gallery of the Sheldonian Theatre in Oxford, England, participating in the World Conference on Church, Community and State, 12-26 July 1937. They had received beforehand the introductory conference papers, the book *The Church and its Function in Society*[9] by J.H. Oldham and W.A. Visser 't Hooft, and the memoranda of the chairmen of the sections. Comprising carefully chosen members from thirty countries, the group was the most representative section of younger leaders which the churches, the World YMCA, the World YWCA and the WSCF had ever brought together internationally in one body. The Youth Commission was also represented at the Second World Conference on Faith and Order in Edinburgh, 3-18 August 1937. Oliver Tomkins was invited to sit in the Youth Commission's meetings as Faith and Order representative on the General Committee preparing for the Amsterdam 1939 Conference.

The impact of the world conferences in Oxford and Edinburgh was felt at the International Christian Leaders' Conference in Sjöstrand, Norway, 30 August-4 September 1938. The main theme of the gathering was "Youth and Ecumenism in Faith and in Action". The secretary, R.H. Edwin Espy, reported that the Utrecht Conference in May in preparation for the proposed World Council of Churches had adopted a constitution for presentation to the churches and had appointed a Provisional Committee to take the necessary steps towards the formation of the Council. The Commission welcomed "the proposal to bring into closer union the Universal Christian Council and the Faith and Order Movement", and expressed its wish "to continue to work through National Youth Committees or representatives which should be free to develop youth work in close cooperation with the responsible church bodies and with the Christian international organizations, until the relationships of Life and Work, Faith and Order and the World Alliance have been finally settled".

The Ecumenical Youth Commission organized from 1933 to 1939 three international essay competitions for youth on the subject "Christ and World Friendship". The contestants were divided into a junior (14-18) and a senior (18-22) group. In response to the first competition 294 essays were received, the second brought 297 essays and the third 328. Most essays were hand-written. Most European languages, including Estonian, Latvian and even Esperanto were represented. There were five essays in Siamese, three in Hova and one in Arabic.

The Ecumenical Youth Commission collaborated with the WSCF and the World YMCA and YWCA in the World Youth Congress Movement which had its headquarters in Geneva. It also cooperated with youth organizations like the International Alliance of Students for Socialism, the International Federation of University Women, the World Community of Youth for Peace, Freedom and Progress, the World Union of Jewish Youth, the Young Communist International and the Young Socialist International. Among the international patrons of the World Youth Congress Movement were the Archbishop of York, the Patriarch of Romania, heads of states and foreign ministers, ambassadors and university professors.

The First World Youth Congress, called by the International Federation of League of Nations Societies, was held in Geneva, 31 August-6 September 1936. The World Youth Congress Movement was established by the 750 delegates from 36 countries attending the Congress, who felt that there was an urgent need for a body which should coordinate the work for peace undertaken by various youth organizations. Soon after national committees were established in many countries. A second World Youth Congress was held at Vassar College, New York State, in August 1938. It discussed: (a) the political and economic organization for peace; (b) the economic and cultural status of youth and its relation to peace; (c) the religious and philosophical bases of peace; and (d) the international role of youth. It developed methods of collaboration to enable the youth of the world to fulfill its responsibility in contributing towards world peace.

Issues of the *Student World* in the thirties give us a sense of the concerns of Christian youth over 50 years ago. W.A. Visser 't Hooft, general secretary of the World Student Christian Federation from 1931-38, was the editor. In the spring of 1937, he wrote in an editorial: "It may well be that many young Christians will become very impatient with the ecumenical movement, because it does not seem that this is enough in a world which needs so much more than words. That is all to the good, if this impatience finds expression, not in pharisaic and negative criticism, but in an attempt to bring the churches (our churches) to a deeper consecration to God's will, which stands for both truth and unity."[10] This was both analytical and prophetic. Youth had indeed experienced the aftermath of the First World War, the years of the great depression and the rising threat of national-socialist and communist totalitarianism in Germany, the Soviet Union and beyond. The world had become more complex, dangerous and explosive in the second half of the thirties than in the previous decades. How could a precarious peace between the nations be maintained?

In the realm of ecumenism there was the struggle to bring together the Faith and Order and Life and Work movements in one international body. The more and the better young Christians became organized, the more they became troubled over the slow pace of progress. Their impatience would become more articulate in the fifties and the sixties. At Amsterdam in 1939 glimpses of truth and unity were caught four weeks before the Second World War broke out.

We must add a word on the involvement of Orthodox youth in the ecumenical movement. John R. Mott had worked intensively for the establishment of branches of the YMCA, the YWCA and WSCF in the countries of the East. During and after the First World War branches of these Christian youth organizations, especially those of the YMCA, sprang up in many places. As a result of Mott's journeys three consultations were held at Sofia in 1928, at Kephissia near Athens in 1930, and at Bucharest in 1933, between leaders of Eastern Orthodox churches and of the World Alliance and of national movements working in Orthodox countries, to discuss the work of the World YMCA in Orthodox areas. While recognizing the independence and autonomy of the YMCA, it was understood that in predominantly Orthodox nations the work of the YMCA should be conducted in harmony with the principles of the Orthodox churches and in consultation with its leaders.

An international conference of Orthodox youth took place at Saloniki, Greece, in November 1930. *Jeunesses orthodoxes*,[11] the official report of this meeting, contains contributions on the problems of the religious life and education of youth by a number of Orthodox leaders. In its resolutions it was stated that modern education responds only partially to the needs of youth in the realms of culture, economics and psychology. The Youth Commission of Life and Work was requested to serve as an international ecumenical agency for the national youth constituencies.

The presence of young Orthodox was strongly felt at the World Conference of Christian Youth at Amsterdam in 1939. Numerically, they exceeded all other Orthodox representations in ecumenical conferences so far. Orthodox youth in fact came into contact with people of other confessions much earlier than their mother churches and they were able to play an active role. At the first WCC Assembly in Amsterdam in 1948, young people were present from the Patriarchate of Antioch and the Orthodox Church of Finland, both not otherwise represented. Vasil T. Istavridis wrote in 1956: "Orthodox youth, within the limits of its potentialities, can aid the work of the mother church in all fields, particularly in the proper placement of the Orthodox within the ecumenical movement and the WCC."[12]

NOTES

[1] *The Stockholm Conference 1925*, official report of the Universal Christian Conference on Life and Work, Stockholm, 19-30 August 1925, ed. G.K.A. Bell, London, Oxford University Press, 1926, p.714.

[2] Constitution and By-Laws, Geneva, Headquarters, 1930, p.3.

[3] *Recruiting for Peace, the World Alliance and Youth*, London, British Council of the World Alliance, 1931, p.3.

[4] Minutes of the meeting of the International Committee, The Hague, 30 September-4 October 1919, p.25.

[5] Records of proceedings of the Eighth International Conference of the World Alliance for International Friendship through the Churches, Cambridge, 1-5 September 1931, p.36.

[6] *Youth and the Church*, report to the Continuation Committee of the Stockholm Conference on Life and Work by its Youth Commission, eds Basil Mathews, Lucy Gardner and Erich Stange, London, Pilgrim Press, 1929, p.17.

[7] *Ibid.*, p.79.

[8] *Ibid.*, p.97.

[9] London, Allen & Unwin, 1937 (Church, Community and State, Vol. I).

[10] Vol. XXX, No. 2, second quarter, 1937, pp.105-108.

[11] Geneva, Editions de la Commission de jeunesse du Conseil oecuménique du christianisme pratique, 1931.

[12] "The Orthodox Youth and the Ecumenical Movement", *The Greek Orthodox Theological Review*, Vol. II, No. 2, 1956, p.88.

II. Amsterdam 1939

The First World Conference of Christian Youth met in Amsterdam in 1939. It was sponsored jointly by the three lay youth organizations — the WSCF, the World Alliance of YMCAs and the World YWCA — and the Ecumenical Youth Commission. Collaborating bodies were the International Missionary Council, the World Sunday School Association, the International Society of Christian Endeavour, and the Continuation Committee which had been appointed by the Second World Conference on Faith and Order at Edinburgh in 1937.

A special conference planning committee, set up in 1935, had decided that half the members of the conference should be representatives of youth groups in the churches, a quarter of the members from the YMCA, and the others from the YWCA and the WSCF. Besides several members of the Ecumenical Youth Commission, leaders of the other three organizations also served on the general conference committee. H.L. Henriod acted as chairman. Several times guests like J.H. Oldham, H. Schönfeld and others were invited to participate. The proposal at first was to hold the conference in 1937 or 1938, but as the WSCF, the World YWCA, the International Missionary Council and the International Society of Christian Endeavour were all meeting in world gatherings in 1938, it was decided to convene the World Conference in 1939.

What was envisaged at an early stage was a smaller world conference of 600 to 800 participants. By 1937 the quota of delegates by countries and movements was fixed. The churches were to send 750 delegates, the YMCA 300, the YWCA 200, and the WSCF 200. Out of 1,500 delegates 42 came from Africa (Angola, Belgian Congo, Cameroon, Egypt, French North Africa, Gambia, Gold Coast, Kenya, Liberia, Madagascar, Mauritius, Nigeria, Nyasaland, Sierra Leone, South Africa, Togoland), 109 from Asia (Burma, Ceylon, China, Dutch East Indies, India, Iran, Iraq, Japan, Palestine, Philippine Islands, Siam, Straits Settlements, Syria and Lebanon, Transjordania), 47 from Australia and New Zealand,

18 from Latin America (Argentina, Brazil, Chile, Peru, Uruguay). There were 17 youth delegates of (the Orthodox Church of) Russia-in-Exile. The leaders, speakers and fraternal delegates numbered 30. There were 44 observers and honorary guests. The age of the delegates ranged from 18 to 35 with one-third over 25.

The general conference had to face the growing menace of war. In the spring of 1939, W.A. Visser 't Hooft was informed by Dietrich Bonhoeffer that war between Germany and the neighbouring nations would soon start, and it would be impossible to hold the conference. Although Germans were forbidden to travel to Amsterdam, a few young Christians from Germany secretly participated in the conference after Visser 't Hooft agreed to let them. Their names did not appear in the list of delegates. The shadow of war made their participation particularly important, and strengthened the solidarity of the members of the international gathering.

Preparing for the Amsterdam conference's programme — subjects, discussion groups, Bible study, worship, special events and features, audiovisual presentations, and local arrangements — the general conference committee circulated an impressive amount of *printed* documents, several of them in three languages, among the 1,500 delegates. English was used in all plenaries and discussion groups. There were a number of French-English and German-English groups and a few with three languages. *Can You Say Christus Victor?*[1] contained ten study outlines on subjects such as: Ecumenism: What is it? Where does it begin? Is there any hope in nations as nations? Is love enough? "But the church can't do anything about anything!" The book, *The Christian Community in the Modern World*,[2] contained several series of questions for use in discussion groups in national areas and an extensive bibliography of current literature. The volume *Further Studies* was widely circulated. *The Faith which Overcomes the World*[3] included twelve Bible studies. The pamphlet *Youth Calls to Youth*[4] was written in order that groups of young people could share in the objectives of the conference through their own thought and action.

Every delegate received a copy of the *Conference Handbook*, a book on *Worship at the Conference*, and the *Cantate Domino* (the WSCF hymnal in its third edition). The *Opening Service, a Service of Preparation of the Holy Communion*, and several other services of worship — in three languages and in printed form — were distributed during the conference. Immediately after the Amsterdam meeting reports of various delegations, such as the Canadian and the Chinese, were circulated. Several main addresses and sermons were separately printed and sent out to participants. On Christmas Day, 1939, the Dutch delegation expressed in a circular letter its faith that "Christus Victor, the only One whom no war can ever vanquish, will keep us united in these dark times", and looked forward to another world conference of Christian youth "as soon as the international situation permits". From the point of view of conference literature and information the World Conference of Christian Youth, 24 July-2 August 1939, was perhaps the most productive youth gathering ever organized.

The main responsibilities of the conference were entrusted to W.A. Visser 't Hooft (conference chairman), R.H. Edwin Espy (conference secretary), H.L. Henriod and Francis House (chairman and secretary for worship services), Suzanne de Dietrich (chairwoman for Bible study) and Tracy Strong (chairman for discussion groups). The daily chairpersons were Madeleine Barot (France), Jean Fraser (Great Britain), Martin Harvey (USA), D.T. Niles (Ceylon), W.C. Lockhart (Canada) and Bengt Redell (Sweden). The conference took place in the concert hall of Amsterdam, the very same place where the delegates to the First Assembly of the World Council of Churches would gather in 1948. "Christus Victor", the main theme of the conference, was not merely a motto; it became a vision and a reality for the participants. For many the theme meant a change of heart, the forsaking of prejudice and an act of courage. It broke down dividing walls of denomination, culture, history and race, and strengthened the hidden bonds of a worldwide fellowship. At the opening session a message from Queen Wilhelmina was conveyed by Prince Bernhard who added in the name of Princess Juliana and on his own behalf a personal word. There was a great rally, in the Ajax soccer stadium, of seven thousand young people who listened to a Russian choir, a choir of African delegates and a number of brief addresses. There was also an evening reception in the historic Rijksmuseum.

In his opening address Visser 't Hooft reminded the delegates that they had not come for "their own spiritual enjoyment" but had to communicate to the multitude of young Christians all over the world that "it is inevitable that unity will prove to be stronger than diversity". In his closing address he challenged the participants to reject "that deepest of all conservatisms, to accept the spiritual status quo of the world", and to see "the dimensions of the plan of God who thinks in terms of the whole world".[5] An achievement of the Amsterdam conference was that it was a forum for discussion and participation and not just a platform for speakers.

Many Americans came to Amsterdam critical of continental theology, and heard the most "continental" speech delivered by Reinhold Niebuhr. He said that Christians ought not to be surprised by the conflicts of the world, which are the result of sin, and that they must not regard the peace of this world as a supreme good. On the other hand, the clearest call to Christian social action was sounded by Pastor Elie Lauriol from France; he dwelt on the need of bread for all humanity. There was an outspoken catholic emphasis in the address of George MacLeod, a Scottish Presbyterian, pointing out that the only real brotherhood is in Christ and in his church. T.Z. Koo from China, at the time a nation devastated by war, spoke on the subject "The Christian Community and the World of Nations". Archbishop William Temple's theme was "In the Beginning, God". John R. Mott urged his listeners to become "ambassadors henceforth to do God's will, come what may". Special interest groups concentrated on seven topics: Christian youth in a world of nations; Christian youth in the nation and the state; Christian youth in economic order; Christian youth and race; Christian youth and education; Christian marriage and family life; the church: its nature and mission.

The first and the last among these had the largest number of participants. The quality of work and reporting varied from section to section. Some participants found themselves in a relatively homogeneous group in which common understanding was reached and much ground covered. Some found themselves in a too abstract and intellectual environment; others judged the discussions in their group to be elementary and superficial. Those who had concentrated on theological preparation, and those who had devoted their energies to the study of practical aspects found little common ground for sharing.

With regard to the first two topics discussed in interest groups, the positive allegiance owed by Christians to the state was for the most part left undefined or taken for granted. While Anglo-Saxons expressed a faith "in the power of honest idealism", Continentals stressed realism and a "reasonable hope for rough justice". All agreed that the problems of colonial empires can be solved and the demands of nations without colonies met only on the basis of Christian principles of justice. Human justice is only approximate. Real justice is based on the fact that human beings are forgiven by God and must therefore forgive their fellow human beings. As the League of Nations has failed to secure peace and justice in international relations, Christians must show that peace includes justice and that they cannot remain neutral on moral issues in international conflicts. Some emphasized that "the church is the conscience of the state", while others felt "that the church's task is simply to preach the Gospel and [it] should abstain from practical action".

Regarding economics, which "used to be considered a dull and dismal science", participants felt that it should become a study of crucial importance. A new economic order must be established because of the great changes which have taken place — "the tremendous increase in population during the last 150 years; unprecedented migration; the development of the capitalistic system with its increase in productivity and the continual discovery of new markets; the reorganization of life on a mass basis; the recent limitations of the previous trend, due to the shrinkage of areas open to colonization; the production of goods in areas formerly regarded as markets and the erection of trade barriers; and technological development".

The unemployment of young people in several countries because of the general depression, the increase of technological efficiency, high birth-rates and a massive exodus from rural areas were matters of grave concern. It was agreed that youth work should not be confined to religious and spiritual matters but should also concern itself with the right use of leisure and the values of physical and recreational activities.

Confronted with the race problem, reports on racial discrimination in religion, education, politics, civil life and economics were presented from Africa (Gold Coast, Kenya, Congo, South Africa), the United States, Australia, New Zealand, the Netherlands Indies and the Federated Malay States. The Jewish problem in Europe was also discussed. "The European who thinks that the South African problem is terrible, and that what happens to the Negroes in the United States is barbaric, tends to forget that Europe's treatment of the Jews is equally uncivilized." The delegates were not willing to go beyond the Oxford declaration on race — and some were not willing to go even as far as that — that the church is "commissioned to call all men into a Divine society that transcends all national and racial limitations and divisions". But there was a need "to work on admittedly bad situations", recognizing that "in discussing the problems a high price must be squarely faced and paid".

In the field of education the impact of radio, cinema, press, the environment, the family, youth organizations, the churches, the Sunday schools and secular institutions of learning received attention. There was no clarity as to the question of what precisely Christian education is; its aims were variously defined. Interesting "practical suggestions were made for producing an ecumenical outlook": to contact Jews in order to gain a new understanding of the Old Testament; to participate in inter-denominational groups between Roman Catholics and Protestants; to send young people and students overseas on an exchange basis; to exchange letters, teachers and ministers between countries and churches; to study the beliefs of other churches; to bridge the gulf which alienates youth from the church.

The last interest group on "The Church — its Nature and Mission" concentrated on the biblical doctrine of the church, its authority, its evangelistic task, its social mission, its approach to the world of other religions, and the way to unity. The hope was expressed "that the World Council of Churches will act as a source of information concerning the faith and order of the various churches". Many felt penitent, humble, disturbed, and were anxious to show the change within themselves by translating thinking into living. "God wills unity. Unity is a call of God, not a choice of man. The unity which he wills involves a return of all churches to their own origins (to their confessions of faith, etc.), and to the central Mystery of the Person of Christ as the Bible witnesses to it".[6]

The two great centres of discovery lay in the Bible studies and worship services. Two hours of Bible study every day for six days was a new discipline to most delegates and proved to be one of the greatest experiences of the whole conference. There was great surprise that the riches of the scriptures had been so little explored, and a sense of bewilderment over the variety of interpretations.

The worship life of the conference left an abiding impression on participants. At the enlarged general conference committee at Bièvres, France, in July 1938, it had been decided that "opportunity must be provided for all members of the conference to share in the fullest expression of the worshipping life of each of the main Christian traditions". Those who conducted worship in the concert hall each day were asked to do so as representatives of the tradition from which they came. During the service in the free church tradition, periods of extempore prayer in French and English expressed praise and penitence, intercession and dedication. The French Reformed service included a message of encouragement and hope to the delegates as they began their discussion of the theme: "The Christian in a World of Conflict". For the Hungarian Lutheran service the platform of the concert hall was arranged like the chancel of a Lutheran church with a great altar table in the centre and a ten-foot cross behind. During a South African Bantu worship a solo Xhosa hymn was sung. A service led by a North American group of young people included Negro spirituals. The opening service was conducted with great simplicity. The Apostles' Creed was recited and the Lord's Prayer said by all. The closing service, conducted by W.A. Visser 't Hooft, consisted of an act of praise and thanksgiving, following a meditation comprising acts of intercession and dedication.

The greatest difficulty was experienced when the problem of different services of holy communion had to be faced. The organizers of the conference felt that the facts of tragic division and isolation should not be blurred. Four main liturgical traditions present were to hold their own services and the whole conference was invited to share in each of them. The service of holy communion meant for the whole conference was held on Saturday night. Robert Mackie, general secretary of the WSCF, pointed the attention of delegates to the fact that, while the need to hold separate services must be a reason, not for irritation, but for penitence, there was in it a real basis for hope. At every celebration of the Lord's supper, Christ is the host, and he calls Christians to strive for the coming of the day when his supper is no longer celebrated in a divided family.

On Sunday morning the holy communion according to the rite of the Church of England was celebrated in the Remonstrantsche Kerk. Ministers from England, America, Japan and India took part in the celebration. The central service of the eucharist was celebrated in the Nieuwe Kerk, one of the mediaeval churches in the Netherlands. The church was full. The sermon was preached by Hendrik Kraemer, and some eleven hundred people partook in the communion.

More than two hundred Lutherans received the communion at the high mass on Sunday evening in the Luthersche Kerk. About four hundred other members of the conference attended the service. The hymns included three by Martin Luther. Non-Lutherans who were present were impressed by the practice of giving absolution individually to each communicant as he or she knelt at the altar steps.

The celebration of the holy liturgy of the Orthodox Church on Monday morning in the concert hall was for most people a totally new experience. Nearly all the delegates were present. English, French and German texts of the liturgy of St John Chrysostom had been provided and the delegates were helped to follow the service by indications on a blackboard. Rev. Archimandrite Cassian Besobrasov, of the Russian Church in emigration, was assisted by Bulgarian, Yugoslav and Russian priests and deacons, all wearing their vestments of purple, or green, or white and gold. Many of the youth were greatly impressed by the Orthodox service.

During the last plenary session it was enthusiastically decided that the cooperative efforts of the five world organizations — the Provisional Committee of the World Council of Churches, the Joint Ecumenical Youth Commission, the World Alliance of YMCAs, the World YWCA, amd the WSCF — should continue; that the possibility of holding another world conference should be explored; that maximum opportunity for full participation of youth must be provided; and that the general secretaries of the cooperating organizations, together with Edwin Espy, should draw up future plans. A meeting of the leaders of the various organizations was scheduled for early spring 1940.

The Lima Conference of 1941, and the steadily growing Christian Youth Movement (Unión Latino-Americano de Juventudes Evangélicas) drew much inspiration from Amsterdam 1939. The United Youth Movement of North America and its affiliated denominational youth fellowships received a tremendous impetus from the same source. As Americans were resolved not to be caught again at so serious a disadvantage in a world conference of Christian youth, serious study of the Bible was introduced into local and area youth conferences. The Student Christian Movement of India, Burma and Ceylon and the student movement in China were strengthened by the spirit and the drive of the first great youth conference. On his return to his country, S.P. Njock Bôt, head of a newly established Christian College at Limbamba in Cameroun, told his friends: "I used to think Christianity was the religion of the white man. Now I know it is the religion of the whole world."

In 1979 Amsterdam 1939 was commemorated in two publications: *We Remember Amsterdam 1939-1979*[7] and *Can You Still Say "Christus Victor"?*[8] The first publication in typewritten form contains 36 contributions; the second publication, a special issue of the *Journal of Ecumenical Studies*, has 41 contributions and 27 short messages from North and South America. In the essays included in the first publication contributors responded to three questions:

1. What are some of the strongest impressions that the Amsterdam conference left with you?
2. What has the Amsterdam conference meant to you in the later years?
3. How can we help those who are at the age we were then to see the ecumenical vision that Amsterdam gave us?

W.A. Visser 't Hooft pointed out in his introductory essay that "nine factors created a situation in which the Spirit could operate:

1. It was an adventure in close cooperation among the various Christian youth movements.
2. The conference reflected the geographical extension of the world Christian community and the cultural variety within it more clearly than any of the large ecumenical meetings had done so far.
3. Amsterdam 1939 was a well-prepared meeting.
4. Amsterdam 1939 became the encounter between the ecumenism of the Christian youth movements and the ecumenism which had more recently arisen among the churches.
5. The conference took place at a crucial moment in the life of the world.
6. The conference took place at a crucial moment in the life of the churches.
7. Bible study had a central place in the conference.

8. Worship was based on the principle of maximum ecumenism.
9. The conference had a strong central message."[9]
Replying to the first and second question, Hendrik Berkhof, from the
Netherlands, made the following observation: "Amsterdam 1939 made
me sensitive to the two great sins of modern society: idolatry and
exploitation". Allan R. Booth from Great Britain noted the commitment
to Christian realism at the conference: "At the moment when we faced the
terrible necessity of resistance, our conference could not take on the
features of pious escapism. We were the generation on whom would fall
the task of fighting for political objectives at the price of our own
survival." In the midst of the human injustice and tragedy, how could the
victory of Christ be proclaimed? "This paradox, the impossible possibility" greatly impressed Kiyoko Takeda Cho from Japan. John White from
Great Britain recalled the use of the ecumenical hymnbook, the saying of
the Lord's Prayer together in over seventy languages and the kneeling at
the altar with the Chinese and the Japanese, their countries already at war.
"The arrangements for worship at most ecumenical conferences in the
period 1948-68 were deeply affected by what happened in Amsterdam in
1939," according to Francis H. House.

Roger and Herrade Mehl from France said: "Certainly there were
theological tensions at Amsterdam: between those who stressed grace and
those who stressed freedom, those who advocated the social gospel and
those who emphasized the eschatological hope, between an introverted
piety and commitment to activism; dialogue was often difficult. But
looking back and comparing Amsterdam (with gatherings) today, it seems
to us there was then a greater measure of unity in affirming the faith
which overcomes the world." For Johannes Verkuyl of the Netherlands
"the enlistment in the ministry of reconciliation between nations, races
and classes" was the highlight of Amsterdam 1939. Robbins Strong's
lasting impression was that "paradoxically, the conference was probably
the most united when it faced together the divisions that prevented us all
from gathering in one place at one time at one Lord's table".

Many American contributions in the *Journal of Ecumenical Studies*
dwell on the enormous changes which have taken place in the world
during the past forty years. The atomic bomb and nuclear energy, at the
time of Amsterdam, belonged to the future. The fate of nations and the
survival of the world were not in the hands of the super-powers. The
planet had not shrunk with jet propulsion and supersonic aircraft. Space
exploration had not begun. Communication satellites, television, instant
replay and computers which have all contributed to the awareness of how
interdependent the human race is, were unheard of. The world of

diplomacy and negotiation and the decision-making processes have since then radically altered, but instant intercommunication has not produced a peaceful world. The spectacular advance of science and technology, ironically, has only accentuated the problems of young people.

Social issues identified in 1939 as concerns of the church have taken entirely new dimensions. Amsterdam did not realize what roles racism, classism and sexism had played then and were to play a few decades later. Threats to the stability of the family as an institution have increased. Divorce, gay rights and the role of the homosexual in the church were in those days not even considered appropriate subjects for discussion. The sixties and seventies were marked by youth's rejection of the "establishment", its search for alternative life-styles and the recourse to drugs.

While the most basic issues of discipleship are the same today as at Amsterdam 1939, some of the political and economic issues are radically new or at least newly apparent. The demands of the two-thirds world for social change to meet the demands for justice are now in the forefront. Very different ideologies as expressed by East-West tensions and North-South conflicts have left their mark on the churches. Only recently have Christian communities become deeply aware of their own cultural conditioning and ideological orientations.

Precisely because of these developments during the last four decades and the consequent withdrawal of youth either into individual pietism or socio-political and economic activism, many participants in the Amsterdam conference in 1939 agreed in 1979 that the passion for unity, so evident forty years ago, needs to be revived. Roswell P. Barnes asks the question as to whether "there is any equivalent background today from which to draw participants for a world conference of Christian youth". How can youth express the conviction "the Christian faith assumes that national, social, ethnic, cultural, and class distinctions do not justify antagonistic divisions before God, that such aspects of the human condition are not barriers within the fellowship of Christians"?[10]

The rediscovery of the quality of unity and the wholeness of the people of God has been greatly strengthened by the singing of powerful hymns from *Cantate Domino*, the multilingual hymnal, originally compiled by Suzanne Bidgrain and issued by the WSCF in 1924, and since then many times revised and reissued as a truly ecumenical and international hymnal. At the Amsterdam conference in 1939, *Cantate Domino* inspired the Czech delegates so much "that, in their isolation during the second world war, they produced a Czech version with words and music, and so felt themselves in spiritual touch with their Amsterdam friends on the other side of the line".[11]

Amsterdam 1939 has been commemorated in many national and international gatherings. At the Vancouver Assembly of the World Council of Churches in 1983, a few of the Amsterdam participants met together. It has been celebrated annually in Japan. Many delegates of the first International Christian Youth Conference became leaders of the ecumenical movement in the next decades.

Before we pass on to the period 1947-54, a few notes on the upheaval, the dislocation, the exhaustion and the depression of millions of people, including the young, caused by the Second World War, may be appropriate. From 1940 to 1945, the World Council of Churches in Formation was unable to function normally through its responsible committees. Until 1942, when the whole of France was occupied, travels and contacts between the Council's Geneva office and Great Britain and the United States were still relatively frequent. But as it proved impossible from that year onwards to hold representative meetings and to share regular information, the members of the Provisional Committee of the World Council met in three groups — in Geneva, London and New York.

The spiritual welfare of the prisoners of war was an immediate concern. The Ecumenical Commission of Chaplaincy Service to Prisoners of War, which was created in 1940, concentrated on organizing active Christian congregations in the camps and providing a pastoral ministry of visitation and counselling. It distributed Bibles, hymnbooks, and religious tracts and secured whatever was needed for the administration of baptism and the Lord's supper. Its work was closely coordinated with that of other agencies — the YMCA, the YWCA, the Bible Societies, the Red Cross, and others. The Department of Reconstruction and Inter-Church Aid, established in 1942, started its work as soon as parts of Western Europe were liberated. It surveyed the needs of churches and Christian organizations which were members of, or cooperated with, the ecumenical movement, brought these needs to the attention of churches which were able to help, and coordinated the projects of aid from one church to another.

The Council's headquarters in Geneva could keep in touch with the countries where the refugee problem had become most acute and, with funds supplied largely by the churches of Switzerland, Sweden and the United States, could organize a ministry of spiritual and material aid, at first chiefly for Christian Jews fleeing from Germany, but also by the end of 1940 for the larger numbers of non-Aryans being deported to southern France. In the same year the CIMADE (Comité inter-mouvements auprès des évacués) was set up by the Protestant youth movements of France. Madeleine Barot was its first general secretary. This organization had one clear conviction: the youth movements must unite in common service to those whom the war had "displaced". Its form of action was to resist, circumvent, bend or break the Nazi laws concerning Jews and other people in every possible way. Many Jews destined to be deported to concentration camps and many others, starving and miserable, were hidden and later rescued from certain death. Jews were "smuggled" across the mountains into Switzerland by courageous young CIMADE workers.

At the end of the hostilities there were almost ten million displaced persons in Europe, several million under the age of 25, to be resettled under the United Nations Refugee Repatriation Authority. In the face of such material deprivation and spiritual isolation, the Council's provisional committee established in 1946 a refugee division in the Department of Reconstruction and Inter-Church Aid under the Ecumenical Refugee Commission, which it had set up at the same time. In the next few years the service to refugees assisted more than 100,000 displaced persons in migrating to new homes and finding employment.

Instead of being a period of stagnation the war years proved a time of deepening ecumenical fellowship. The delegates to the World Christian Youth Conference at Oslo in 1947 were deeply moved and newly committed when they heard of the stories of sacrifice, love and heroism of fellow Christians during the years of conflict and devastation.

NOTES

[1] By Eward F. Quellette, a study outline based on the World Conference of Christian Youth, Amsterdam 1939.
[2] By W. Walter Gethman and Denzil G.M., Patrick, a preparatory study for the World Conference of Christian Youth, Geneva, Conference Headquarters, 1939.
[3] Bible studies compiled by W.A. Visser 't Hooft and Suzanne de Dietrich, London, SCM Press, 1940.
[4] By H.W. Fox, outlines for study on Christian youth in the modern world, London, British Christian Council, 1938.
[5] *Christus Victor*, report of the World Conference of Christian Youth, Amsterdam, 24 July-2 August 1939, ed. Denzil Patrick, Geneva, Conference Headquarters, 1939, pp. 148-149 and 15.
[6] *Ibid.*, pp.46-145 passim.
[7] "Forty Years After the First World Conference of Christian Youth", mimeographed.
[8] Ed. R.H. Edwin Espy, in *Journal of Ecumenical Studies*, Vol. 16, No.1, winter 1979.
[9] *Ibid.*, pp.3-7.
[10] *Ibid.*, pp.117 and 114.
[11] Ruth Rouse, "Other Aspects of the Ecumenical Movement, 1910-1948", in *A History of the Ecumenical Movement, 1517-1948*, London, SPCK, 1954, p.632.

III. Oslo 1947
to Evanston 1954

At the meeting of the Provisional Committee of the World Council of Churches, held in Geneva from 21 to 23 February 1946, W.A. Visser 't Hooft sought its approval to set up a Youth Department of the Council. He reported that, since Edwin Espy, the secretary of the Ecumenical Youth Commission, had to return to the United States at the beginning of the war, the position of ecumenical youth secretary had remained vacant. Many delegates at the Amsterdam Conference had expressed the wish that a second conference should be held as soon as possible after the war. There had already taken place a joint meeting of representatives of the youth organizations concerned, when it was agreed to hold a second world youth conference in 1947. Two other bodies had expressed their interest, the International Missionary Council and the World Sunday School Association. The reason for choosing the year 1947 was that the organizations were anxious not to lose altogether the war generation; they did not wish to give the impression that the initiative in youth work had been taken over by political or semi-political bodies.

The World Sunday School Association was founded at the convention in Rome in 1907. In 1947, it adopted the name World Council of Christian Education. In 1950, the words "and Sunday School Association" were added to the name. In 1971, the Council merged into the educational structure of the World Council of Churches.

It was obviously necessary, according to the general secretary of the World Council, to appoint an executive officer to prepare for the conference and it was desirable that this officer should be on the staff of the Council. The decision was taken to invite Francis House, who had considerable experience in youth activities in the SCM and the WSCF and had recently worked for the World Student Service Fund and the Federation in Greece. He was succeeded in 1947 by Jean Fraser.

The Provisional Committee approved the setting up of a Youth Department of the World Council with a special committee of its own, and outlined its task as follows: (a) to serve as the centre of ecumenical contact and inspiration for the youth movements directly related to the churches; (b) to collaborate with the international Christian youth movements and other Christian agencies concerned with youth in ecumenical youth activities.[1]

The Youth Department was commissioned to represent the World Council of Churches on the World Christian Youth Commission. This body, representing the World Alliance of YMCAs, the World YWCA, the WSCF and the World Council of Christian Education and Sunday School Association, organized the Second World Conference of Christian Youth at Oslo in 1947. The name "World Christian Youth Commission" was formally adopted a year later, indicating their desire to work together whenever possible. The same body also sponsored the Third World Conference of Christian Youth in 1952, at Kottayam, South India.

Later, in 1966, the International Catholic Conference of Guiding, the International Young Christian Workers, the International Young Catholic Students, the World Federation of Catholic Youth, Pax Romana (International Movement of Catholic Students), and the International Movement of Catholic Agricultural and Rural Youth joined the Commission.

At the meeting of the Provisional Committee of the World Council of Churches in Buck Hill Falls, Pennsylvania, in April 1947, William Keys reported on the immediate plans of the Youth Department, especially on the plan to make a world survey of the church youth movements, in collaboration with the World Sunday School Association, on the preparation of the Oslo conference and the participation of youth in the Amsterdam 1948 Assembly. He also mentioned the relationships with the Reconstruction Department, and the proposal to add to the Youth Department a secretary for reconstruction. The Provisional Committee approved a statement of policy for the Youth Department.

It took eighteen months of hard work to prepare the programme, to publicize the event, to raise travel funds and to choose the delegates to the Oslo conference, 22-31 July 1947. Various publications were circulated before the meeting. Ten pamphlets of preparatory study material were printed in three languages on the following topics: (1) How is Christ overcoming the world? (2) Who decides what is good and evil? (3) Does the Bible help us to know how to act? (4) Is man the slave of his inventions? (5) Must individual freedom and social justice clash? (6) Must society be built upon the family? (7) On what basis is world order possible? (8) Are the churches beyond repair? (9) Can the churches really unite? (10) Can the church avoid being utopian or escapist?

Rowena Ferguson, Associate Editor of *High Road*, was commissioned to write *Christian Youth in the United States*.[2] The Youth Department of the British Council of Churches published *Can the Churches Work Together?*[3] An elaborate *Conference Handbook* was compiled in a trilingual edition. Several worship services and morning prayers during the conference were distributed in printed form. After the conference *The Chief Speeches at Oslo*,[4] including addresses by W.A. Visser 't Hooft, D.T. Niles, M. Barot, K.F. Mather, R. Niebuhr, Chu-Wen Li, M. Niemöller, Bishop E. Berggrav, R.S.K. Seeley, Alex Johnson and Bishop E. Rohde, was published by the Christian Literature Society in Madras. Mabel Small and Norman J. Bull published *Oslo Calling*[5] on behalf of the Youth Department of the British Council of Churches. R.H. Edwin Espy compiled *Christianity as a Youth Movement*,[6] which included several evaluations of youth movements in various countries.

The 1,200 delegates of the conference were chosen on the following basis: World Alliance of YMCAs, one quarter; World YWCA and WSCF, each one eighth; WCC and World Sunday School Association, one half. Besides Australia, New Zealand, Canada and the United States, 15 countries from Africa, 18 countries from Asia, 15 countries from Latin America and 21 countries from Europe were represented. It was a difficult task to mobilize the delegates, to finance their journeys and to bring them to Oslo at a time of considerable restrictions on travel. The conference chairman was Alex Johnson; deputy chairman R.C. Mackie; the conference secretary Francis H. House. Oliver S. Tomkins was in charge of the worship services, Gerald Cragg of Bible studies and Edwin Espy of discussion groups.

"Oslo had naturally not quite the same quality of adventure and pioneering which has characterised Amsterdam, but it had something else: a combination of sobriety concerning the realities of the world situation with the grateful recognition of the Lordship of Christ over His whole Church and over the world".[7] Setting the stage for the meeting, W.A. Visser 't Hooft, in his opening address in the Filadelfia Hall, spoke of the claim made by the theme: "Jesus Christ is Lord".

In the second plenary address, on the theme "The Lord of the Bible in History", D.T. Niles emphasized the fact that the Bible is not so much concerned with ideas about God as with God himself, that the Bible does not simply set forth God but is the place where God comes to meet us. Reinhold Niebuhr's address "Man's Disorder and God's Design" was later the theme of the First Assembly of the World Council in 1948. "The root of all disorder is in *ourselves*... This does not, however, allow us to contract out of social guilt... We live in the tragedy of a culture which states that it is moving away from disorder into higher possibilities when all the time it is only moving into higher forms of disorder."[8] Kirtley Mather, a scientist from Harvard University, spoke on "Confronting Self-sufficient Science". Today for the first time in history, he said, human beings have the power to commit mass suicide and destroy civilization. The great decisions we must make are not in the realm of physics and chemistry but in the realm of morals and religion.

In discussing the subject "There is a World Church", Chu Wen Li of China acknowledged that everything in the church situation today seemed to deny the statement. Madeleine Barot spoke on "Confronting Moral Chaos".

The opening service of worship took place in the Vaar Frelsers Kirke cathedral where Bishop Eivind Berggrav ministered. In his sermon he gave a testimony from the depths of his experience during the occupation — his defiance of Vidkun Quisling, who attempted to convert the church, schools and youth to national socialism, and his own resignation, with all the bishops and most of the clergy, from every form of office under a police state, and their imprisonment. The morning and evening services were conducted according to various denominational liturgies, including a service of the Evangelical Church of the Czech Brethren and a service prepared by Miss Kyoto Takeda Cho from Japan. On Sunday the High Mass of the Norwegian Lutheran Church was celebrated. Ninety per cent of all members of the conference accepted the invitation to communicate, as baptized members of their own churches. On Monday morning Metropolitan Pantaleimon of Greece celebrated the eucharist.

The celebration of St Olaf's Day on 29 July was a special event. Olaf, the first Christian king of Norway, fell at the battle of Stiklestad in 1030. He was later declared a saint. The cross became the symbol of the Norwegian flag.

Almost thirty-thousand people participated in a rally in the Bislet Stadium. Another special feature was a world broadcast, which enabled members of groups at home, from which the delegates had come, to join in the activities of the conference. Daily press conferences were held and Christian leaders from many countries were interviewed on crucial questions.

The conference was divided into thirty-five groups, both for Bible study and discussion. The Bible studies were outlined in a booklet by Suzanne de Dietrich. Since the delegates remained in the same groups throughout, there was close relationship between the Bible studies and the discussion sessions. In every case the leader in charge of the Bible study attended the special subject discussion and vice versa. The topics of the discussion groups were the following: (A) freedom and order; (B) Christian responsibility in a secular environment; (C) world order; (D) man and his inventions; (E) the family in the community; (F) the Christian congregation's life in the local community; (G) education in the modern world; (H) the Christian faces the situation of the Jew; (I) the church faces the world.

The Second World Conference of Christian Youth did not adopt an official message. It was felt that the delegates themselves were the message as well as the messengers, and should convey the spirit of the assembly to others. A spirit of repentance and reconciliation marked the conference. The very day the meeting began, fighting had broken out between the Dutch and the Indonesians. In a statement on Indonesian-Netherlands relations it was pointed out that "the lack of true spiritual concern, of passionate prayer and of true Christian unity" contributed to the situation. It affirmed "the right of the Indonesian people to liberty and independence".

Later during the conference the French issued a declaration on the whole colonial question. They maintained that all colonial policy should be aimed towards making subject peoples ready for independence; they thanked God that their conversations with delegates from French colonies were marked by an authentic spirit of friendship. The representatives from Great Britain and India rejoiced that India was on the threshold of independence. German delegates met with representatives of the countries which Germany had occupied during the war. There were meetings of American delegates with delegates from the Philippines, for a long time under American control.

At a consultative conference in Lund, attended by 100 delegates from 40 countries, work on the constitution for the Youth Department was completed. It was affirmed that the Department was and remained a department of the WCC, and that the question of direct affiliation of church youth movements to the Department did not arise, since they were related to the Council through the churches to which they belonged.

At the First Assembly of the World Council of Churches in Amsterdam, 1948, Philip Potter presented a statement on behalf of the youth delegation. A hundred young people from forty-eight different countries, of whom many were also present in Oslo, attended the Assembly. Among the key sentences in the statement are these: "We cannot express too strongly how pained we are by the divisions of the churches. At every point in our discussions... we are brought up against the inability of the churches to be clear and authoritative... because of their disunity on the basic issue of the nature of the Church... We are convinced that the time has come when the churches must speak of each other in love of the stumbling-blocks which mar our fellowship and which drive men and women, and especially youth, away from us... We need not so much ecumenical understanding as ecumenical obedience... The evangelization of the young people cannot be attempted by the senior members of the churches without the young people, or vice versa... We cannot resist the hope that at the next Assembly not only will there be a larger representation of laymen and laywomen, but that young people will be included as delegates and guests."[9]

The youth delegates felt that the following problems should be stressed in the study commission and appropriate dialogues started: (a) the worldwide struggle between liberalism and communism; (b) the colonial problem; (c) the rights of minorities; (d) racial theory and colour discrimination; (e) atomic power; (f) human rights; (g) whether the church as such can directly intervene in political affairs.

From Amsterdam 1948 to Evanston 1954 the Youth Department was directly related to the General Secretariat of the Council. Staff persons in the department were Jean Fraser (director), William Keys (secretary in New York), Jan Mirejovsky (secretary for European reconstruction), and George Booth (director of work camps). Other departments of the Council then were: International Affairs, Inter-Church Aid and Service to Refugees, Study, Faith and Order, Evangelism, the Ecumenical Institute, the Commission on the Life and Work of Women in the Church, and the Secretariat for Laymen's Work.

A conference of European leaders on youth reconstruction held at Présinge, Switzerland, in October 1947, prepared a considerable programme to increase spiritual resources and aid in the development of youth work in many countries. Aid for this programme came from several countries outside Europe, but to an increasing extent channels of mutual aid were being discovered in Europe itself. Jan Mirejovsky, with the help of Inter-Church Aid, was responsible for the programme.

From October 1947 at Présinge until November 1954 at Crêt-Bérard, eight European youth leaders' conferences were held (see Appendix II). Though more countries were represented at the second conference in November 1948, Belgium, Czechoslovakia, Finland, Norway, Poland, Sweden and Yugoslavia were unable to send their leaders. Leaders' training became the most important concern in youth work. The term most in use was "personalization of ecumenical relationships". A scholarship programme was initiated. At the first meeting the problem of industrial youth was discussed; at the second gathering the question of rural youth came to the forefront.

Robert Mackie, the director of Inter-Church Aid and Service to Refugees, elaborated on the necessity of an effective sharing of resources. Reconstruction work must lead from one act of love to another. If one member of the body is in difficulty, the whole church suffers. He also reminded the gathering that there is much agony and suffering outside Europe, in particular in Asia, and that priorities of financial support to young people need to be worked out. Visser 't Hooft emphasized that if confessions are not constantly re-examined, or modified as new light breaks from the scriptures, churches could become isolated, static and unrepentant, unable to receive gifts from others. Both real unity and real division demand church-centred youth work and independent interdenominational youth work.

Viewing the whole situation in Europe anew, the third youth planning conference at Présinge in November 1949 struck a particularly sombre note. The pre-war Europe was gone. A simple return to the situation "normal" had become impossible. The continent's spiritual, moral and social structures were weak and even sick. The problem of a new Europe was not basically economic and political, but religious. Nobody knew yet what the continent's shape would be.

Several annual youth conferences which were held in the Hendrik Kraemer House from 1952 to 1956 were especially concerned with contacts with the German Democratic Republic and other countries in East Europe and were so timed that participants from the West had an experience of the May Day parade and the government pressure on young Christians. These gatherings took so much time for planning that Jean Fraser pressed European youth leaders to assume greater responsibility.

The 1950 listing of youth projects included the following nations and emphases: Austria, Czechoslovakia, Finland, France, Germany, Greece, Holland, Hungary, Italy, Spain, Orthodox in France and other countries. The total amount sought was $146,700, of which $63,400 went to Germany, $17,010 to Italy, $15,200 to Hungary, $10,940 to Greece, and $10,890 to Czechoslovakia. Germany received $23,000 in addition for food, Austria $3,000, Greece $2,000 and Czechoslovakia $1,900.

Ecumenical work camps were a well-known and regular feature of the Youth Department since it began work in 1947. It was in the beginning an American initiative, much supported by Ray Pitsker who assisted the Youth Department for several months. Until the end of the fifties some 10,000 campers from over 60 countries and various confessions participated in 387 camps in 47 countries. (This is the total figure including American work camp programmes.) In the late fifties there was a

significant expansion of ecumenical youth camps in Africa, Asia and
Latin America, and national work camp committees had to be created.

In the late forties a considerable number of campers were delinquent
young people. The leaders of the camps had to guarantee to the prison
authorities that none of the young would escape. Refugee and homeless
youth also participated in camps. The types of projects were as varied as
the young campers themselves. In Germany campers helped clear the
rubble and erect homes for refugees, poor students and delinquent youth.
In France a sewerage line over one kilometer long was dug through the
rocks and dirt of the Cévennes plateau where a Protestant school had been
started as an experiment in Christian education and community life. High
in the Alpine region of Northern Italy over 200 young people working
through three summers erected a building dedicated to the love of God
which knows no frontiers, and the place was called "Agape". The
Waldensian Church sponsored here several ecumenical youth gatherings.
Amazed Japanese citizens watched youth from America and Korea
clearing land for a children's playground in a repatriate centre. Some
groups worked as long as nine hours a day with pick and shovel. Bible
study, group discussions, trips to spots of social significance —factories,
refugee camps, prisons — or of historic interest, visits to nearby churches, help to needy families in the neighbourhood, all these were on the
camp agenda.

The question was often asked: "What makes these camps specifically
ecumenical, and why are they part of the programme of the World
Council of Churches?" Experience showed that the peculiar genius of the
ecumenical work camps lay in the fact that:

a) they were an occasion for young people of different confessional
    backgrounds to live, work and worship together for some four weeks,
    and thus to experience the common life in the body of Christ, and to
    become aware of their responsibility to work for the unity and the
    renewal of their own churches;

b) they helped the campers through work and worship to understand
    anew their calling as "fellow workers for God", and to gain a clearer
    conception of the relevance of their faith to their everyday life;

c) they enabled young people to be confronted with the actual social,
    economic and political issues with which the local community had to
    wrestle;

d) they were a training ground for the ecumenical encounter which the
    campers had to enter in their home countries and communities.[10]

When We Work Together, a booklet compiled by William A. Perkins,
reflected the excitement and the challenge of ecumenical work camps. He

wrote in the introduction: "Leaky tents, hard beds, strange cooking, unusual customs — these combined with hard work, worship, study, and community living make work camps one of the most adventurous activities of Christian youth today. This voluntary service involves sacrifices of time that could be spent in a profitable summer job, and of money to pay to go to and from and to work in a camp. Getting to know people of different backgrounds, whether in an international setting or your own town, demonstrates that personal encounter is the way to understanding and reconciliation. Voluntary work proves that young people are not satisfied to accept the *status quo*. Many are willing to be different in order to do something about it."[11]

By the 1950s there was a change in emphasis. The first work camps stressed a pick-and-shovel involvement in relation to post-war reconstruction and rehabilitation, but in 1953, with the first camp in Sweden, the camps began to emphasize community service. The shift in emphasis became even more evident in the 1960s (see chapter VI).

The fourth European youth planning conference was the occasion for Bengt-Thure Molander from Sweden to take over the work from Jan Mirejovsky who had been recalled to Czechoslovakia. Miss Fraser outlined the proposals which had been made for a closer relation between the Youth Department and the Service to Refugees in their work for young people. She emphasized that this was not designed to develop any special service for young refugees, but rather to give them the same opportunities ecumenically that were available for other young people. At the previous meeting she had reported that fifteen hundred young people crossed every day from Eastern to Western Europe. Some of them were afraid that they would be sent to work in the uranium mines in the East or in Siberia, others were driven out because of lack of work, or came in the hope that conditions would be better in the West. Twelve hundred young people crossed the German border into France each month. The teams of CIMADE had helped them with papers, to find work or opportunities for study, and also to bring them into relation with church life.

As already mentioned, the YMCA and the YWCA were engaged from 1945 onwards in an extensive service programme for displaced persons (DPs) and refugees, generously supported by the churches, especially those in the United States. This ministry to uprooted youth was undertaken without regard to nationality, race, creed, class or political affiliation. The workers insisted on meeting refugees where they were and helping them to overcome their own problems. Refugee and non-refugee staff were recognized as equal members of one team. Many key positions were later filled by young displaced persons who had found a sure and

significant new place in life. Both organizations worked in close coopera-
tion with the International Committee of the Red Cross, the League of
Red Cross Societies and United Nations organizations like the United
Nations Relief and Rehabilitation Agency (UNRRA), the Office of the
High Commissioner for Refugees (UNHCR), and the International
Refugee Organization (IRO).

At the fifth European youth planning conference relations with international organizations were discussed. There was some confusion as to
whether Christians should work primarily *in* or *with* intergovernmental
and non-governmental bodies.

Much of the attention of the sixth planning conference was focused on
the preparation for the Third World Conference of Christian Youth in
Travancore, India, for which the World Christian Youth Commission
carried the major responsibility. Besides hearing and discussing progress
reports on world youth projects, work camps, mobile teams, leadership
training, confessional youth movements, the seventh and eighth consultations of European national youth secretaries in 1953 and 1954 concentrated on the preparations for and the follow-up in connection with the
youth delegation to the Evanston Assembly. At the seventh consultation
Visser 't Hooft spoke of youth as "the loyal opposition within the
church", a theme which continued to be discussed through the decade. It
was suggested that in 1955 one youth conference in Berlin should take up
the race question and another in great Britain should deal with Faith and
Order matters.

The Third World Conference of Christian Youth at Kottayam, Travan-
core (now Kerala), India, 11-25 December 1952, was attended by 350
delegates from 55 countries and 28 confessions. Ms Sarah Chakko from
India was the chairman of the conference planning committee, and K.M.
Simon the organizing secretary. The conference leader was Prof. Laksh-
man Perera from Ceylon. The Bible study coordinators were Marie-
Jeanne de Haller and Stanley Samartha. The secretary for groups was
Bengt-Thure Molander. Addresses were given by Sara Chakko (India),
Tsunegoro Nara (Japan), Annie Baeta (Gold Coast), Martin Niemöller,
Leo Marsh and Visser 't Hooft. They dealt with the variety of ways in
which God's call comes to men and women and they respond to it. Paul
Limbert represented the World Alliance of YMCAs; Helen Roberts the
World YWCA; Philippe Maury the WSCF; Wilmina Rowland the
WCCE; W.A. Visser 't Hooft the WCC; and Norman Goodall the IMC.
Fraternal delegates came from the Baptist World Alliance, the Interna-
tional Congregational Council, the World's Christian Endeavour Union,
the World Convention of Churches of Christ, the World Methodist

Council, the World Presbyterian Alliance, the Salvation Army World Office, the United Bible Societies, the Boy Scouts International Bureau, the World Association of Girl Guides and Girl Scouts, and the United Nations.

The conference was clearly an Asian enterprise in that sense, not to be compared with the two preceding world gatherings. Two-thirds of the delegates came from Asia, the Middle East and the South Pacific. Most meetings took place in a *pandal*, a temporary structure with a thatched roof supported by bamboo poles. The young people learned to associate the *pandal* with public ceremony, worship and theatrical performances.

The delegates discovered that Asia was not the changeless East, a symbol of all that is ancient and static. Political independence had brought hope to many, but had also raised for them acute social and economic problems. Communism had already become the ideological creed in many parts of Asia and young people were increasingly being attracted to it. The old faiths of Asia were in a renascent phase.

Every evening a mass meeting was held at a public square in Kottayam, which attracted wide attention and was reported in the press. The conference shared in the life of the community on the occasion of St Thomas's Day, 20 December, which commemorated St Thomas who, according to tradition, arrived in India in 52 A.D. Delegates attended services in the churches of Malabar — Syrian Orthodox, Syrian Jacobite and Mar Thoma — and in the Church of South India which was the result of an organic union of Anglicans, Methodists, Presbyterians and Congregationalists in 1947. There was, however, no service of holy communion at which all delegates could participate. In a town where the Syrian Orthodox Church was predominant, the question of an "open" communion service could not arise.

As the theme of the conference was "Jesus Christ the Answer — God was in Christ Reconciling the World unto Himself", the following topics were submitted to the discusison groups: (1) Interpreting the gospel of Jesus Christ; (2) Jesus Christ and the search for personal freedom; (3) the church's witness to Jesus Christ; (4) the claims of Christ in personal and family relationships; (5) Christ in a world of tensions.

The main difference of opinion which surfaced was around the nature of the church. It was agreed that the church is part of the gospel but there was no agreement about how the church is to be identified in history. "Where in fact is the true church to be found? What is the relation of the churches as they actually exist to the church which Jesus Christ founded?" It was generally felt that "the true community of the 'koinonia' is revolutionary in character. The church must become a place where human worth and common responsibility are actualized... Creative love must express itself not simply in acts of mercy, genuine and important though they may be, but in attempts to achieve a more just economic and social order."[12] Discussion groups dwelt on the Muslim opposition to the gospel on grounds of doctrine, the Buddhist suspicion that Christian evangelism is a front for political and cultural imperialism, and the Hindu claim that Hinduism provides for the expression of the best in all religions. The gospel of Jesus Christ needs to be reinterpreted to adherents of renascent historical religions, believers in the basic equality of all religions, scientific relationalists, Marxists, and the indifferent.

The exchange of letters between the conference delegates and communist youth leaders brought into focus the critical issue of communism's challenge to the youth of the world. The dialogue dealt with the problem of war and peace, arms reduction and a ban on the use of atomic, bacteriological and chemical weapons, social liberation and justice, the question of racial discrimination, protection of women's rights, etc.

Nine workshops, conducted by experts in each of the respective fields, demonstrated ways of making the study of the Bible relevant to the daily life of young people; helping youth to enter into the worship of the churches; building and conducting programmes with a variety of interests that appealed to youth and securing a measure of continuity in them; teaching the value and use of music for young people; preparing and displaying filmstrips, posters, and other visual aids; expressing ideas through drama; orienting activities to rural life; planning and managing work camps, caravans, and service projects in towns and villages; writing for newspapers on religious subjects; and producing literature young people would appreciate and use.

The Youth Department cooperated with the Ecumenical Institute at Bossey in arranging a 12-week course for youth leaders in summer 1947 and a three-week course in April 1948. Such courses became a permanent feature of the Institute's programme in the fifties. The principal emphases in the training in ecumenical life for young people were: (1) missionary: the appeal to make the church effectively worldwide; (2) putting into practice what the Study Department does in theory; (3) the concern for Christian unity, a process related to the work of Faith and Order; (4) development of a sense of Christian responsibility in social and political affairs, in which many young Christians were still notably lacking; (5) development in areas where the ecumenical spirit is weak; (6) in Europe, relations with Inter-Church Aid, which will always be a necessary part of the ecumenical movement; (7) unity and common purpose.

In a consultation on leadership training held by the World Christian Youth Commission in September 1953, the Youth Department partici- pated in defining the new essentials of training for leadership in youth work under the following heads: Bible study, worship, the Christian mission, the Christian movement, personal relationships, the Christian in society, leadership of youth, and the organization and administration of youth work.

In her report to the WCC Central Committee at Chichester in 1949, Jean Fraser stated that the purpose of the Youth Department was to remind the churches of their responsibility for youth, and youth of its responsibility to the ecumenical movement. The question was raised as to whether there could not be youth representation on the Central Com- mittee. It was explained that this would require action by the Assembly itself. Visser 't Hooft pointed out that the Committee could invite consultants to attend its meetings and it was possible to include young people in the category. Ten young people attended the Bangkok Confer- ence of the Eastern Asia Christian Conference in 1949, and twenty young people took part in the third World Conference on Faith and Order at Lund in 1952.

A world study of church youth work,[13] mentioned earlier, was carried out from 1948 to 1950 by Evert Stowe for the World Council of Churches, the World Council of Christian Education and the International Missionary Council. It reflected the policy of the World Council of Churches' Youth Department to secure maximum youth representation at all major ecumenical gatherings. Evidence from many parts of the world showed that there was a new consciousness on the part of churches themselves of the needs of youth, and an awareness that these needs were not being met by much of traditional church life. New forms were being tried out, and full-time workers appointed to guide the churches in their youth policy. Some 200 replies were received to a questionnaire sent out in May 1948. In many instances the replies reflected the thought and the information of a group rather than of a single individual. There were various reactions to an article of Emil Brunner from Switzerland, entitled: "The Christian Message for Postwar Youth", which contained seven main points: (1) youth needs the gospel; (2) does youth want the gospel?; (3) the gospel is preached but not interpreted; (4) identifying the gospel with youth's aspirations; (5) the gospel interpretation must be gradual; (6) evangelization may start with Christian fellowship; (7) the personal approach must be revalued.

Existing programmes of youth work in Europe, Asia, Africa, South Pacific and the Americas, special aspects of activities and methods in leadership training, and organizations in denominational and non-denominational church youth work — all these were described in the study. In reply to the question of the needs of youth the following problems were most frequently mentioned: sex, marriage, the home; social and political problems; vocation, and a philosophy of work; cultural relations and problems. The study was a valuable instrument for the Youth Department to discover its role in different areas of the world.

A conference of Orthodox youth at Bossey in January 1949 expressed the conviction that the Orthodox youth movement's special task was to bring to the church young people who had lost their faith or were indifferent to religion. It was felt that youth movements in all the autocephalous churches should have direct relations with one another in order to exchange their experiences. Orthodox youth should be prepared to explain those dogmas which were not clearly understood by other Christians, especially the place of Virgin Mary in the life of the church. The conference elected a continuation committee, composed of A. Schmemann, N. Nissiotis, H. Georgiadis and P.L'Huilier. At a congress of Orthodox youth of Western Europe in Sèvres, near Paris, 7-12 April 1953, SYNDESMOS (Bond) was founded, in which young people from France, Greece, the Middle East and Finland participated. During the next year two national meetings took place in Germany and Great Britain. SYNDESMOS is the only international Orthodox youth organization. General assemblies have been held in France, Greece, Lebanon, Sweden, USA, Switzerland and Finland.

The functions of SYNDESMOS are: (1) to be a bond of unity between Orthodox Christian youth organizations throughout the world and to set up such organizations wherever possible; (2) to promote among them a deeper understanding of the Orthodox Christian faith and a common vision of the tasks of the Orthodox church in the modern world; (3) to foster relations, cooperation and mutual aid between them in the realization of these tasks; (4) to assist Orthodox youth in their relations with other Christians and people of other faiths; (5) to be an instrument of furthering cooperation and deeper communion with the Oriental Orthodox churches through common youth activities.

The General Assembly of SYNDESMOS meets every three years, the Executive Committee once a year. This world fellowship has implications for Orthodox witness in general and fosters ecumenical relations, in particular with the World Council of Churches, the Ecumenical Youth Council in Europe, the Conference of European Churches and the Middle-East Council of Churches.

The eleventh assembly of SYNDESMOS at Castelli, Crete, 14-19 August 1983, was attended by some 200 people from 29 countries. The central theme was "Unity and Mission". It worked through six commissions: unity, theological education, pastoral mission of the church, education of the people of God, missions and ecumenical relations. The assembly approved a main theme for the period up to 1986: "The Church, a Eucharistic Community", which calls attention to the fundamental structure of Orthodox life. Six new youth organizations were accepted as members. At present SYNDESMOS has 46 members in 24 countries.

A convention, held by the World Council of Christian Education at Toronto, 10-16 August 1950, around the theme: "Confronting the Contemporary World with Jesus Christ — Teacher and Lord", worked in four sections on the Christian education of children, youth, adults, and on the total task of Christian education. A study guide was prepared for use throughout the world. Of the 1,000 participants 80 per cent came from the United States and Canada. Major attention was paid to the problem of industrial youth, as this topic was the concern of the World Christian Youth Commission between 1950 and 1952. The discussion also centred on ecumenical cooperation at international, national, and local church levels.

At the Third World Conference on Faith and Order, 15-28 August 1952, youth consultants were active participants.

Two commissions of a consultation on "The Place and Function of Youth Work in the Church" at Bossey, 27 April-3 May 1953, discussed the questions of confirmation and preparation for church membership, and of Christian youth as they face the problems of the world.

The Youth Department published the *News Sheet* six times annually from October 1947 to June 1955. Some 2,500 copies were sent to the offices of member churches, to national correspondents and individual subscribers. Besides the regular editorials by Jean Fraser, the *News Sheet* contained much information on conferences and consultations, on the ongoing cooperation with the YMCA, the YWCA, the WSCF, and the WCCE, on work camps, and regional, and national developments in youth work around the world.

NOTES

[1] The World Council of Churches in Process of Formation, *Minutes and Reports*, meeting of the Provisional Committee, Geneva, WCC, 1946, p.42.
[2] Nashville, Tennessee, 1947.
[3] A study outline for youth groups based on Christian witness in the post-war world, London, British Council of Churches, 1947.

[4] Addresses at the World Christian Youth Conference, Oslo, July 1947, Madras, Christian Literature Society, 1947.

[5] The story of the Second World Conference of Christian Youth, Wallington, Surrey, Religious Education Press, 1947.

[6] For *Highroad* (Methodist Youth Journal of Religion), 1947.

[7] *The Ten Formative Years 1938-1948*, report on the activities of the World Council of Churches during its period of formation, Geneva, WCC, 1948.

[8] *Report* of the Second World Conference of Christian Youth, Oslo, 22-31 July 1947, ed. Paul Griswold Macy, Geneva, Conference Headquarters, 1947, pp. 176, 177, 197.

[9] *The First Assembly of the World Council of Churches*, Amsterdam, 22 August-4 September 1948, ed. W.A. Visser 't Hooft, London, SCM Press, 1949, pp.184-187.

[10] *Evanston to New Delhi, 1954-1961*, report of the Central Committee to the Third Assembly of the World Council of Churches, Geneva, WCC, 1961, p.96.

[11] New York, Friendship Press, 1960, pp.5,27,31,39.

[12] *Footprints in Travancore*, report of the Thrid World Conference of Christian Youth, 11-26 December 1952, Coonor, Nilgiris, India Sunday School Union, 1953, pp.59,60 and 75.

[13] *World Study of Church Youth Work,* summary of information and judgments concerning youth work of the churches, London & New York, World Council of Christian Education and Sunday School Association, 1951.

IV. Evanston 1954
   to New Delhi 1961

This chapter deals with European youth planning conferences, youth leaders annual consultations, several consultations on specific themes, and the Ecumenical Youth Assembly at Lausanne in 1960, which was a regional European meeting. All these gatherings were related to one another and closely followed each other.

At the Evanston Assembly in 1954, the Youth Department was given a new constitution. It became a department within the Division of Ecumenical Action, together with the Department on Laity, the Department on the Cooperation of Men and Women in Church and Society, and the Ecumenical Institute in Bossey. This modification strengthened the Youth Department in its efforts to promote ecumenical education and in helping the churches to accept young people as active participants in their life and witness. It also meant working under a new discipline and a certain limitation of its freedom.

The Department shifted its accent from the development of ecumenical councils and from preoccupation with world conferences to a more concentrated emphasis on the evangelization and the nurture of youth. This meant giving greater attention to the needs of the teenage group, in addition to the older 18-30 age group. In view of the vast increase in the youth population of the world, greater emphasis was laid on regional developments and on closer cooperation with other world bodies.

The Assembly at Evanston was reminded of the fact that many young people leave the church at an age when they should be taking up responsible membership in churches. At the meeting of the Central Committee in Davos, Switzerland, August 1955, Bengt-Thure Molander spoke in his report "of the high value young people set on ecumenical experience, and of the encouraging advance made by church-related youth movements in a number of countries". He continued: "But the main present concern of the Department arose with the problem of integrating young people into the life of their churches. Millions of young people completely lost touch with any church after their confirmation. The Youth Department felt that the time had come to try to deal with the problems systematically by providing opportunities for those concerned with them to share their feelings and experiences."

The Youth Committee presented a statement to the Central Committee which contained the following significant paragraph: "In attempting to face all the issues involved in the common failure to integrate youth fully into the worshipping and witnessing life of the church, we have all been challenged to reconsider the very nature of our youth work in the light of the present mission of the church in the world and in view of the sociological and psychological problems of adjustment which young people must undergo as they grow into adulthood in the world today. Indeed, we have been forced to rethink, in this context, both the evangelistic task of Christian youth itself, and the nature of the preparation for full church membership carried out by the churches and of the commitment carried out by young people."[1]

At the meeting of the Central Committee in New Haven in 1957, the question was raised as to "how the church can integrate young people into her life without taking them out of the world?" In the report of the Youth Department it was stated that "youth no longer fits into the structure of the church" because of the rapid and radical changes in society. It was added that in certain countries "experiments in new ways of open non-directed youth work are being made in order to reach youth who are not closely related to the church".[2]

Immediately after the meeting of the Central Committee at Davos, a youth Faith and Order consultation was held at Canterbury from 25 August to 1 September 1955, under the leadership of Edward Patey, youth secretary of the British Council of Churches. The consultation discussed five concerns: (1) the relation of Christ and the church; (2) the nature and problems of ecumenical worship; (3) world confessionalism and ecumenism; (4) Christian lay youth movements and the church; (5) the relation of Faith and Order to ecumenical concerns. Surprisingly the question of intercommunion did not figure prominently in the debate.

Following up the Davos Central Committee decision to engage in a study on "The Integration of Youth in the Life and Mission of the Church", the Youth Department sponsored two special consultations, both in Holland, on "Baptism and Confirmation" in 1958, and on "Holy Communion" in 1960. The consultation at Hilversum, 6-11 January 1958, was attended by 25 youth leaders from several countries in Europe, representing nine confessions, under the guidance of J.K.S. Reid, who gave four major talks on the biblical background of baptism and confirmation.

Participants in the consultation at Driebergen, 11-15 January 1960, struggled with the theme "Holy Communion and Youth". Among the leaders were Keith Bridston, Max Thurian and Hendrik Berkhof. Again, the question of joint celebration of the eucharist was not debated in Driebergen. There was an apparent weariness about the problem of intercommunion.

It was at the Ecumenical Youth Assembly at Lausanne, in 1960, that the problems which arise when it is not possible for all the members of a conference to receive holy communion together were highlighted. A consultation on "Services of Holy Communion at Ecumenical Gatherings" was held at the Ecumenical Institute, Bossey, 1-4 March 1961, under the auspices of the Youth Department and Faith and Order. The first part of the findings dealt with proposals for the revision of the recommendation of the Lund Conference on Faith and Order concerning services of the eucharist at ecumenical gatherings. The second part was submitted to the WCC member churches, especially those which had sent delegates to Lausanne in 1960, and to various ecumenical bodies. It dealt more generally with the question of intercommunion in the light of the developments since the Lund conference.

The most important recommendation submitted to the Faith and Order working committee suggested that a host church "should be encouraged to invite all members of the conference to receive the communion at its service, even though all will not be able to receive, and though some may conscientiously object to the holding of open communion services" and that there should be "special emphasis both on the note of penitence for our continued separation from one another and on our given unity in Christ".[3] In a separate paper, added as an appendix to the findings, Max Thurian drew attention to an essay by T.F. Torrance in the volume *Intercommunion* and to his suggestion that "to refuse the Eucharist to those baptized into Christ Jesus and incorporated into his resurrection-body (i.e. the Church) amounts either to a denial of the transcendent reality of Holy Baptism or to attempted schism within the Body of Christ".[4]

The following seven questions were addressed to the member churches of the WCC:

1. What are the implications of membership of the WCC?
2. Have the churches re-examined their rules of communion discipline in the light of the new ecumenical situation?
3. What advice about participation in communion services is now to be given by the churches to those who take part in ecumenical gatherings under the auspices of the WCC?

4. What does communion at ecumenical gatherings mean?
5. What are the reactions of the churches to the spontaneous developments in intercommunion that are taking place?
6. What is the responsibility of the churches for ecumenical education?
7. Do the churches take steps to heed the message of ecumenical gatherings?[5]

Besides several consultations in Berlin on specific themes, such as the "Race Question" (1955), "Stand Fast in the Faith" (1956), and the "Christian Community in a Changing World" (1957), the WCC Youth Department together with the Youth Department of the British Council of Churches sponsored a third youth Faith and Order consultation at Lincoln, Great Britain, 16-20 January 1961, on the theme "Youth and Evangelism".

During this period six more consultations of European youth secretaries were held in Switzerland, Holland, Germany and Sweden, which dealt with the planning and follow-up of consultations and conferences, regional developments, work camps, world youth projects, cooperation with other ecumenical bodies and relations with national organizations, staff visits, staffing of the department, and finance. Every one of these meetings faced the challenge to reconsider the very nature of youth work in the light of the contemporary mission of the church in the world and of the sociological and psychological problems of adjustment which young people undergo as they grow into adulthood in modern society.

At the annual consultation in Oud Poelgeest, Holland, 10-15 October 1955, papers on the integration of young people in the life and mission of the church by B.T. Molander, N. Steenbeek, H. Visser, H.O. Wölber, R. Kempes and F. House were presented and discussed. It was decided to constitute a "brains trust" to help European national correspondents to pursue further the study on the integration of youth.   .

At the consultation of European national youth secretaries in Crêt-Bérard, 5-12 October 1956, Hans-Ruedi Weber led a Bible study on the mission of the church. In his address on the "World Council of Churches' Concerns", Visser 't Hooft argued that there is a movement only when the churches pass from egocentricity to a true concern for all the churches, and from an uncritical identification of themselves with any nation or race to a sense of *una sancta* which transcends nation and race. In his address "Towards Christian Youth Responsibility in Contemporary Affairs", Philip Potter called for a radical revision of Europe's attitudes towards the rest of the world. He expressed the hope that the youth will become aware of the grave danger of identifying with what the New Testament calls *pleonexia* — wanting to annex more, or "grasping self-assertion".

After the consultation at Hamburg, 7-12 October 1957, national correspondents spent two days evaluating the answers received to the questions in relation to the study of "Integration of Young People in the Life and Mission of the Church". The questions were:

1. What steps must be taken to promote a more effective relationship between ministers, youth leaders and the young people with whom they are concerned?
2. Is it the primary function of youth work to establish separate youth communities within the parish, or is it to enable young people to take part in the total life of the local church?
3. What is the place of the "open" group in a parish? How can the church through an open group meet the spiritual, no less than the material, social and intellectual needs of the youth within it?
4. In Christian youth work what is the right relation between the *didache* (instruction in the Christian faith and life) and the *kerygma* (the presentation of the gospel)? Should the one precede or follow the other?
5. What is the relationship between human *fellowship* and Christian *community*? What are the practical implications of this theological question in Christian youth work?
6. How does our disunity as churches hinder the task of integrating young people into the life of the church? What new insights does the ecumenical movement bring to this whole question?
7. How can the church integrate young people into her life without taking them out of the world? Do not all answers need to be re-examined in the light of this great question?

The next two annual meetings at Crêt-Bérard, 28 October-1 November 1958, and at Sigtuna, Sweden, 15-17 November 1959, were concerned with preparations for the European Youth Assembly at Lausanne and the new relationships with the World Council of Christian Education and Sunday School Association (WCCESSA). After the inception of the WCC Youth Department in 1946, it was learnt that WCCESSA was considering setting up its own youth department with similar aims. Following much discussion in 1947 it was decided to establish such a department and when, in 1950, a full-time youth secretary was appointed a closer cooperation between the two bodies developed. There was a large overlap of the members of the committees of both departments, so that up to the time of Evanston there was a great deal of common planning and action. The cooperation was particularly important for the Youth Department because the WCCESSA was greatly concerned with the work of youth under 18. It also strengthened the ties with the churches in the United

States, because the WCCESSA was strongly rooted there. After Evanston the youth secretary of WCCESSA resigned and his post was not filled. The portfolio for youth work was carried by the associate general secretary of that body, with office in New York.

A committee of the WCC/WCCESSA Youth Departments was established, and met at Herrenalb, Germany, 19-23 July 1956. It discussed thoroughly the relations between the two departments. The two central issues related to who should administer the world youth projects and how far its programmes and budget should be extended. It was decided that a joint WCC/WCCESSA secretary should be appointed to administer the scheme, spending part of his time in New York and part in Geneva. The committee emphasized that world youth projects need to be closely related to the whole work of the Youth Departments and of the Division of Inter-Church Aid, and that there should be careful consultation with that department before any radical extensions were made.

It was also decided that the Youth Department should continue its policy of encouraging local ecumenical groups to take over the planning and administration of the work camps, particularly in Europe, that practical efforts should be made at every work camp to prepare the young people for that sudden disillusionment which often comes when they return to face all the bitter denominational divisions in their home situations after their exciting experience of real ecumenical encounter, and that the work camps should be a place where Christians could confront people of other faiths, challenging and testing the faith of each other.

There was further discussion on the responsibility of Christian youth in political matters. The committee reaffirmed a statement made at Taizé, in 1953, that while the WCC Youth Department would not establish relations with world youth organizations (other than Christian organizations and the UNESCO), nevertheless church youth groups in each country must decide on their responsibility in relation to such organizations, and that the Youth Department had the definite task of helping young people to think through the social and political consequences of their faith.

Tokyo was the venue for the fourteenth World Convention of Christian Education, 6-13 August 1958. The first World's Sunday School Convention was held in London in 1889. In 1950 there were 437,338 Sunday schools and 37,387,384 teachers and students.[6] The Tokyo Convention was preceded by the second World Convention on Christian Education near Kobe, 19 July to 1 August 1958, in which a professional group of 300 people shared some of the concerns and methods of Christian education. The first World Convention on Christian Education took place in Toronto in 1950.

The work of the commissions of the second World Convention on Christian Education was preceded by four major addresses: "Christian Education Faces a World of Rapid and Bewildering Social Change" (Christian Baeta); "Christian Education Faces the Individual's Responsibility to Live as a Christian in his Community" (Enrico Sobrepena); "Christian Education Faces the New Interest in the Bible Through New Translations and Discoveries" (Marshall C. Dendy); "Christian Education Faces a Deepened Awareness of the Importance of Christian Theology" (Sante U. Barbieri).[7] There were two related meetings; a meeting of the joint youth committee of the WCC/WCCE and a consultation of Asian youth leaders, sponsored by the joint youth committee and the East Asia Christian Conference. "Jesus Christ, the Way, the Truth, and the Life" was the theme of the Japan meetings.

From 1955 to 1960, 262 ecumenical work camps were organized in various parts of the world, involving some 5,650 work campers. Fifty-three camps registered over 1,200 young people from 36 countries in 1961. Although the Division of Inter-Church Aid and Service to Refugees financed the camps, their organization remained under the supervision of the Youth Department.

In the late fifties there was a significant expansion of ecumenical work camps in Asia, Africa and Latin America. An extensive staff visit in 1959 in Asia, where camps had been sponsored since 1949, led to the beginning, in 1960, of annual work camp leaders' training conferences, similar to those held regularly in Europe and the United States. While up to Evanston only one camp had been held in Africa, since then some 16 camps were organized there under the auspices of the Youth Department. As the sponsor of the largest number of international work camps, the Youth Department was represented on the Coordination Committee for International Voluntary Work Camps related to the UNESCO. Staff members attended special UNESCO consultations, in India in 1958 and in Yugoslavia in 1960.[8] These consultations were annual, and the one in India was the first outside Europe. William A. Perkins served several years as vice-chairman of the coordination committee.

World youth projects figured in the Youth Department's report at Evanston as part of its programme. The projects were based on needs which had to be met through the development of church youth work in a country and they served as a stimulus for self-support. There were five kinds of activities which were facilitated by world youth projects: leadership training, literature for youth work, visits of leaders between countries or continents, the establishing of youth centres, and the provision of full-time interdenominational youth workers.

Jointly sponsored by the WCC/WCCESSA youth departments, 33 projects involving 24 countries were initiated in 1959. Of these 13 were for leadership training, 9 for erecting camp and conference centres, 7 for assisting the secretariat of ecumenical youth councils and 4 for publications. In 1960, 30 projects from 23 countries were carried out. All these helped to establish closer contacts between Christian youth in various countries, through correspondence, and through the publication of three valuable booklets, *When We Pray*[9] compiled by Wilmina Rowland, *When We Share*[10] compiled by Frances Maeda, and *When We Work Together* compiled by William A. Perkins.

Youth voluntary service was a programme which responded to the numerous requests received from young people who desired to give voluntary unskilled service whenever it was needed. These requests led the Youth Department in 1957 to be involved in a refugee programme under the auspices of the Division of Inter-Church Aid and Service to Refugees. Until the end of the fifties 135 young people from 12 countries and 13 denominations had served through this programme in refugee homes in Austria. The success of the experiment led to the exploration of other fields for such service and a beginning was made in the placing of youth volunteers in the service of CIMADE. Only 50 volunteers could be taken in 1960, in spite of the large number of offers. The Youth Department was in close touch with organizations which required volunteers. In February 1960 a consultation on voluntary service was held under the auspices of the World Christian Youth Commission, bringing together leaders of several international agencies working with youth volunteers.

The General Committee of the WSCF, meeting at the Evangelical Academy of Tutzing in 1956 with strong delegations from the younger SCMs, took the decision to inaugurate a new programme of conferences and publications on the theme "The Life and Mission of the Church". The leaders of the Federation —notably D.T. Niles and Philippe Maury — believed that an "ecumenical consensus" had emerged about the revealed nature of the gospel and the missionary nature of the church. "The programme was designed in order to educate students in this theological consensus, and in order to train them for the mission to the world. But as the project developed, the cries of a revolutionary world almost drowned the dynamic simplicity of this original message, and the ecumenism which had emerged in the Federation countless words later was no longer neo-orthodox: it was radical."

The World Teaching Conference at Strasbourg, 16-31 July 1960, was addressed by some of the church's ablest speakers, like Karl Barth, D.T.

Niles, Visser 't Hooft and Lesslie Newbigin.[11] But in spite of the eloquent lectures the audience was restless. "There seemed to be too much speaking about the life of the church; what students wanted was action in the world. And there seemed to be too much mission; what students wanted was a welcome to this world".[12]

Charles Long, carrying responsibility for the project on the life and mission of the church, wrote six months later in an article "An Attempt to Sort Out a 'Whirled' Conference": "Quite a few of us may still look back on those weeks of July 1960 as a nightmare and a terrible storm of impressions which, on first reflection, we feel fortunate to have survived. Only slowly are we beginning to realize in what ways we have been permanently marked by the experience. I feel this will eventually be seen as a point of crisis in the history of the church, a tornado that gathered persons, convictions and conflicts from the four corners of the earth."

His theological conclusion was that "in and through the world God is present to men and crucified by men. The coming of Christ was a secular event and will always be a secular event. When we confuse 'alienation from the Church' with 'separation from God', we deny both the reality and the efficacy of Christ's cross and resurrection. God in Christ has once and for all laid claim to the world and shown the extent of his love for it. Literally nothing in the world can separate us from that love. Nothing can be placed beyond the range of his redemption, neither by the agnosticism of modern man nor by condemnation by the Church nor by the indifference of Christians. This is *God's* world."

The positive results of the Strasbourg conference were that it "began to sketch the outlines of a new geography of unbelief, and in doing this the majority of the participants accepted as a fact that the Church has come to the 'end of the foreign missionary era', especially in the sense that professional missionaries will soon cease to be a Christian caste enjoying special privilege and honour within the Church, and carrying the burden of Christian witness in pagan lands to the ends of the earth". Strasbourg also represented a revolt against globalism. The disillusionment was expressed not only with the structures of the churches, but with the structures of the ecumenical movement, including the WSCF. This was balanced by the conviction that "the mission and the unity of the Church are simply abstractions unless they become real in the local Christian communities where we live".[13]

In retrospect the meeting of the general committee of the WSCF at Tutzing in 1956 is seen as marking new emphases in many areas of work. It was increasingly clear to many SCMs that the rapidly changing nature of the university in a technological age, the changing relation of the university to society, the widening gap between the "two cultures" — "the literary intellectuals" and "the scientists" — the increasingly secularized societies, and the ambiguous situation in current theological thought were all confronting the Federation and its member movements with new challenges and new responsibilities at every level of the educational process. As the WSCF had started to establish SCMs in many third world countries, the concern for political discussion by students on struggles for independence became central. The "racial revolution" was well on its way. The internationalization of universities became in itself a process of "inter-racialization". Christian students in the United States participated actively in sit-ins, freedom rides and voter registration campaigns. Apartheid in South Africa received much publicity and provoked much opposition. An openness to relationships with national and international secular organizations, particularly in East Europe, was regarded as a matter of Christian witness. The emphasis from speaking *to* young people of other convictions was shifted to conversing *with* them.

The Ecumenical Youth Assembly at Lausanne, 13-24 July 1960, was held under the auspices of the Youth Department and the national ecumenical youth committees in the different European countries. Its main theme was "Christ, the Light of the World", the theme of the forthcoming Third Assembly of the World Council of Churches in New Delhi, 1961. There were some 1,800 participants, with delegations from the churches in Poland, Hungary and Yugoslavia, and "delegated observers" from the Moscow Patriarchate, the Baptist-Evangelical Union in the USSR and other churches which were not members of the World Council. There were also officially approved observers from the Roman Catholic youth movements in Switzerland. The majority of the delegates were not university students. The average age was 22.

The assembly tackled three themes: "The European Churches in the World Situation Today" (speakers M.M. Thomas and N. Nissiotis); "The Task of the Churches in a Changing European Situation" (speakers R. Mehl, T. Driberg and W. Gastpary); "The Renewal Mission and Unity of the Local Church" (speakers E. Lange and H. Hoekendijk). The major part of the time was spent in 60 discussion groups, with 25 delegates in each. The assembly had received a generous contribution of $30,000 from the Swiss churches and considerable help from the WCC's Division of Inter-Church Aid for delegates from overseas and from Eastern Europe. A feature of the assembly was a week-end spent in visits to parishes all over French- and German-speaking Switzerland. All main sessions took place in the spacious Palais de Beaulieu.

The findings of the assembly, prepared by a group of delegates, with Ernst Lange serving as secretary, contained several frank and critical statements. Emphasized in these were the selfish acquisitiveness of Europe, the necessity of lowering its standards of living, and the need for sending young technicians, engineers and agriculturalists, and not only missionaries, to third world countries. The shameful inability to join together in holy communion was deplored.[14]

The French delegation drew up a statement with regard to the political situation in Algeria and expressed the desire "that the French Government take up again the negotiations with the representatives of the FLN with a view to an early ending of hostilities and to the free and impartial application of the principle of self-determination". Addressing the people of Switzerland, the Swiss delegation proposed "to encourage the youth and young adults to practise their profession during a period of 3 to 5 years in countries in the process of development, whether as farmers, technicians, engineers, teachers or specialists of any kind".[15]

In his closing address, Philip Potter, director of the Youth Department, remarked that to his knowledge this assembly was the first ecumenical gathering which had placed such a strong emphasis on the local community and the local church. Later, reporting to the Central Committee meeting at St Andrews, Scotland, in August 1960, on the deliberations of the Ecumenical Youth Assembly, Philip Potter asked for a re-examination of the status of a gathering of this kind, where baptized believers, delegated by their churches, met in Christ's name to study the Bible, to think together about their obedience as Christians in the world, and experience a living community in the Holy Spirit.

The strongest words during the conference were spoken by Hans Hoekendijk. He asked: "Are there no revolutionaries here? People who do not want to improve or to modify the structures and institutions of our Christian life but who are ready to break out of these prisons...? Is there any chance for you to avoid one of the major ecumenical sins, that is, to be churchy...? Are you going to deal with the issues of unity in your local situation in an impatient and recklessly courageous way?"[16]

It is not difficult to assess the Youth Department's concentration on "The Integration of Young People in the Life and Mission of the Church" — the objective adopted, as we may recall, following the Evanston Assembly. From 1960 onwards the word "integration" was replaced by "critical participation" and youth was to move into the sixties by expressing quite different concerns and pursuing more radical objectives than the established churches.

In 1954 it was suggested that the *News Sheet* change into the format of a small magazine carrying not only news of ecumenical youth work but more substantial articles. While this new format had been well received since it came out in 1955, it was difficult to continue its publication for long. The Youth Committee then proposed that the *News Sheet* be replaced by the following: (a) more youth news included in the *Ecumenical Press Service*; (b) a bulletin published twice a year on definite subjects, similar to the *Laity Bulletin*; (c) occasional books or pamphlets on important issues; (d) pamphlets or brochures on the work of the Youth Department. In 1960 it was again decided to publish a new organ called *Youth*. Ten numbers were published until the end of 1964, and these contained original and valuable contributions.

NOTES

[1] *Minutes and Reports*, Eighth Meeting of the Central Committee of the World Council of Churches, Davos, Switzerland, 2-8 August 1955, Geneva, WCC, 1955, pp.46-47.

[2] *Minutes and Reports*, Tenth Meeting of the Central Committee of the World Council of Churches, New Haven, USA, 30 July-7 August 1957, Geneva, WCC, 1957, pp.99-100.

[3] *The Ecumenical Review*, Vol. XIII, No. 3, April 1961, pp.355-56.

[4] "Eschatology and the Eucharist", in *Intercommunion*, eds Donald Baillie and John Marsh, London, SCM Press, 1952, p.339.

[5] *The Ecumenical Review, op. cit.*, pp.361-63.

[6] Gerald E. Knoff, *The World Sunday School Movement: the Story of Broadening Mission*, New York, Seabury Press, 1979, p.164.

[7] *Report of the World Institute on Christian Education*, 19 July-1 August 1958, Seiwa and Kobe Colleges, Nishinomiya, Japan, New York, WCCESSA, 1958.

[8] News Sheet of the Youth Department, November 1956 and No.4, 1958.

[9] New York, Friendship Press, 1955.

[10] New York, Friendship Press, 1957.

[11] *The Ministry of Christ and Our Calling*, a thematic summary of quotations from the major lectures and papers presented to the World Teaching Conference on the Life and Mission of the Church, Strasbourg, 1960, Geneva, WSCF, 1960 (WSCF Document 1599).

[12] David L. Edwards, "Signs of Radicalism in the Ecumenical Movement", in *The Ecumenical Advance: a History of the Ecumenical Movement*, Vol. 2, ed. Harold E. Fey, London, SPCK, 1970, p.400.

[13] Charles Long, "An Attempt to Sort Out a 'Whirled' Conference", *Student World*, Vol. LIV, Nos 1-2, 1st and 2nd quarter, 1961, pp.19-25.

[14] *Youth*, No. 2, October 1960, pp.81-87.

[15] *Ibid.*, pp.89 and 91.

[16] "The Renewal Mission and Unity of the Local Church," *Youth*, No. 2, October 1960, pp.65-67.

V. Two Decades
of Regional Developments

When the World Council of Churches was inaugurated in 1948, the non-Western delegates at the Assembly had mixed feelings. They were afraid that the newly created body would have a Western orientation. Among the 351 official delegates at the First Assembly there were 26 from Asia, six from Africa, three Latin-Americans, one from the Near East, and none from the Pacific. The Amsterdam statements about unity disappointed the Indians who, less than a year before, had seen the inauguration of the Church of South India. D.T. Niles of Ceylon, who served the Youth Department as chairman from 1948 to 1953, expressed their feelings when he said: "The older churches were discussing the reasons and circumstances which had led to their earlier divorce; the younger churches were only just getting married and did not wish to be asked their opinion on the subjects which had led to the quarrels between the older churches."[1]

The world confessional families — now called the Christian World Communions — at one time played an ecumenical role. They gave the members of their churches a certain sense of universality through mediating the worldwide character of their fellowships. Many of their leaders participated in the formation of the World Council of Churches and held positions of leadership in it. Despite the efforts to make the WCC an instrument of the churches in all continents, and not of confessional movements, P.D. Devanandan confessed in 1951: "Some of us from the so-called younger churches left Amsterdam with a heavy heart, because we could not help feeling that somehow we did not belong. The entire trend of discussion veered round problems of life and thought which primarily concerned the older churches. Moreover, we gained the impression, rightly or wrongly, that we were being made to think and act in accordance with ideas, doctrinal and political, which are current in the older churches."[2]

This came partly from a strong confessional loyalty at that early stage in the life of the WCC. Confessional representation was more important than regional representation. Delegates from the younger churches continued to raise the question whether the Council should not take into account the inter-regional aspect of the ecumenical movement, instead of concentrating on interconfessional ecumenism. Behind their concern was the conviction that the church should become truly catholic (out of all the nations) and truly missionary (sent to all the nations).

In the area of youth work, during the period after Evanston a much greater emphasis was placed on regional developments.

The following account of regional youth developments in Asia, the Middle East, Africa, North America and Latin America are to be seen in the light of the earlier and later preoccupations of the Youth Department. The growth of the WCC, the increasing autonomy of European ecumenical youth councils and national work camp committees, and the changes in emphases of the Youth Department paved the way for a more systematic involvement in youth work in other continents and regions. A conscious decision was made not to hold world Christian youth conferences but to promote regional assemblies and conferences. The Ecumenical Youth Assembly at Lausanne in 1960 was a regional gathering. It was a turning point in ecumenical service to youth as a whole and its impact was in a short time felt worldwide.

Asia

At the conference of Christian leaders of East Asia, in Bangkok in 1949, nine young people from Japan, Korea, the Philippines, Malaya, Indonesia, Indo-China, Siam, Ceylon, India and Pakistan were brought together to discuss the extension of WCC work in Asia. The discussion emphasized the fact that the work of international bodies there — the YMCA, the YWCA, and the Student Christian Movement, for example — touched mainly those in educational institutions who could speak the English language, and that the needs of the majority of young people in the churches called for special attention.

Reporting on the Bangkok conference and on her various travels during 1949 and 1950, Jean Fraser wrote in *The Ecumenical Review* that "the whole face of Asia has been changed, and youth has been the instrument of that change".[3] She noted "the disrupting of old patterns and social habits through the removing of thousands of young men from their villages... Their horizons are no longer limited by the paddy-fields that they can see from their thatch houses: they have been in touch with the world of machines, where change is a possibility. This has exactly the same effect on their minds as the first impact of scientific teaching has on the mind of the student. 'The acids of modernity' eat into the structure of the traditional faiths. Once religious sanctions have been flouted with success in the name of some scientific agricultural method, the whole religious structure begins to crack. The younger generation is getting loose from its moorings and no longer responding to the ancient religions."

This left the field wide open for communism, which promised to do away with poverty, and to give individuals a sense of their historic importance. The churches, in most places a small minority, were not sure of their place in the nationalist struggles and in movements for social and economic justice. There were recent efforts to organize young men's Muslim associations, young men's Buddhist associations and Hindu movements of young people, a sign of religious resurgence in the wake of national awakening. Christian teaching in schools was being prohibited in many places, and governments were increasingly assuming responsibility for school and university education. In many cases churches were going through a time of acute identity crisis. One of the encouraging signs, however, was the remarkable growth of Christian youth councils. The conference at Oslo in 1947 had given Christian youth of Asia a vision, a message, and a renewed confidence in their evangelistic task. The results had been noteworthy in Indonesia, the Philippines, Japan and Korea. In India and Ceylon youth councils were already related to the national Christian councils, and had greatly increased the scope of their concern. In a number of cases, however, they had been unable to augment their activities, due to lack of money and adequate staff.

Miss Fraser continued to travel widely through Asia during the next few years — to Ceylon, Burma, West Pakistan and Malaya. It was decided that she should make her headquarters in India for fifteen months prior to the Kottayam conference in December 1952. Under her leadership consultations of youth workers were held both in North and South India, and also a three-month training course for youth leaders with the purpose of developing forms and methods of youth work close to Indian life.

A youth committee of the National Christian Council of India and Pakistan was set up in 1949, in which the YMCA, the YWCA, the SCM, the India Christian Endeavour, the India Sunday School Union, six church youth organizations and six provincial youth committees were represented. The committee succeeded in making the Christian youth conscious of the ecumenical heritage of the church with special reference to youth movements. It organized a Christian youth conference at Allahabad, which brought together two hundred delegates from India,

Pakistan, Burma and Ceylon representing all important youth organizations. The theme of the gathering was "The Call of the Hour".

A consultation on youth work in South India, at Bangalore, 2-4 June 1953, and a consultation on youth work in North India, 1-2 July 1953, both under the auspices of the Central Youth Committee of the National Christian Council, discussed (a) youth work in the churches and its relation to other youth organizations; (b) effective youth programmes in the church; (c) youth work in villages; (d) Christian vocation; and (4) sex, home and family life.[4]

The scope of the work of the central youth committee of India grew steadily. A national Bible study programme was developed jointly with the YMCA, YWCA and SCM. In the early sixties the need was felt for observing on the national level one Sunday in the year as a youth Sunday. A string of city youth councils was created across India to further the ecumenical movement at the local level. Recognizing that a knowledge of the culture and language of youth was a prerequisite for the effective presentation of the gospel, a Delhi urban ecumenical youth project was formed, and it received much attention. Mathai Zachariah, the secretary of the central youth committee, wrote in an interpretative report in 1964 that the major task is "to search for the real situation of youth, to study its culture as it finds expression on the Indian scene with its new 'language', and 'myths' and symbols, and to find out what exactly the gospel is for them…"

In Burma, the Burma Christian Youth Council struggled unsuccessfully to establish satisfactory relations with the All Burma Christian Youth League and the Burma Youth Council. Bertrand and Daisy de Luze from France had already reported in 1949 that the Baptist churches in Burma felt little need to have links with other Christians and were fearful of any kind of "super-organization".

According to U Kyaw Than, who had served as associate general secretary of the WSCF and then as IMC-WCC East Asia secretary, "while young people in the West are often reported as being frustrated, bored and without hope, the Asian young people, because of the present developments in their history, are full of excitement and expectancy. A whole new world lies in front of them." He added that "there is a general consensus among the churches that a new emphasis must be made on the Christian nurture of the young people as they grow into responsible adulthood".[5]

Youth work in Ceylon was carried out in many local parishes by the four major Protestant churches, the Church of Ceylon, the Methodist, Baptist, and Presbyterian churches, with a loose central organization. The

YMCA, the YWCA and the SCM were active in a few centres. A particular problem was that the church membership was largely drawn from middle-class communities. The deep gap between the English-educated middle-class Christian youth and the poorly educated youth in the villages, speaking only Sinhalese or Tamil, was difficult to bridge.

Singapore formed a Christian youth council as a coordinating body. Apart from the YMCA and the YWCA, the only Christian youth organization to have a coordinated youth programme under a paid secretary was the Methodist youth fellowship, with its 35 chapters in Malaya. There was no direct contact with Roman Catholic youth except indirectly through the Singapore Youth Council.

Organized youth work in Thailand started slowly. A joint committee on youth work was formed by the American Presbyterian Mission and the Church of Christ in Thailand. The committee held seven consultations in which 400 young people participated. Young peoples' societies were formed in many local churches.

The Christian youth fellowship of the Presbyterian Church was the only organized youth activity in Formosa. Cooperating in the National Ecumenical Youth Council of Indonesia were church youth organizations of several denominations, the SCM and the YMCA. The Japan Union of Christian Endeavour, the YMCA, YWCA and SCM were represented in the youth commission of the National Christian Council of Japan. Related to the National Christian Council in Korea, the National Council of Youth was supported by the Presbyterian, Methodist and Holiness Churches and the Salvation Army. The main problems faced by the youth committee of the West Pakistan Christian Council, in which both churches and missions participated, were illiteracy, poverty, unemployment and the growing number of intercommunal marriages.

At an Asian youth work consultation at the International Christian University in Mitaka, Tokyo, Japan, 2-6 August 1958, sponsored by the World Council of Christian Education, the WCC Youth Department and the East Asia Christian Conference, several reports on national situations were presented and discussed. A sharp and unfortunate separation between rural and urban youth in the churches was noted. Christian education material was primarily prepared for the university and high-school student groups. Trained leadership was lacking in rural areas. The consultation explored ways to improve the relations between national councils of churches, the WCC/WCCE Youth Departments and the lay youth organizations. Church leaders were encouraged to further the ecumenical movement and to make key personnel available for ecumenical youth work.

The archives of the WCC library contain some scattered documents and records on youth in China before and after the revolution in 1949. A report, *Christian Youth in China*, written by C.W. Li in 1947, emphasized the magnitude of the task of post-war reconstruction in that nation. Practically no corner of the vast country had remained unaffected by suffering, death and devastation. But in spite of great discouragement, the youth saw signs of hope for the future. In places like Shanghai, Peiping, Nanking, Canton, Amoy and Foochow youth meetings were held again after eight years of occupation. New student associations were organized and old ones revived. The publications of various Christian youth movements were resumed. There was a large Chinese youth delegation at the Oslo 1947 conference.

Between 1949 and 1952, YMCA, YWCA, SCM and the local parishes had ceased to function. In Peking in June 1954, a national congress was attended by 150 students and 120 young pastors from various denominations. Their theme was: "Who is Jesus Christ?" A message was sent to the government. Mao Tse-Tung replied with "a confession of non-belief in the Christian faith", but considered that "the church which grows on the soil of China is a part of our national patrimony", and must be granted the necessary freedom. Young people had a large stake in rebuilding the church. There were some three million Protestants in China. Controversy with communism was considered impossible and undesirable. Young Christians were convinced their daily actions alone must prove their loyalty to Christ in the new situation.

The first conference of the Youth Department of the Philippine Federation of Christian Churches was held in Cebu City in March 1948, a second in Manila at the end of the same year. A quarterly, *Filipino Christian Youth*, provided articles and topics for group discussions. Youth fellowship activities, summer service projects and work camps were developed. The Asian Christian Youth Assembly at the Silliman University, Dumaguate City, took place from 28 December to 8 January 1965. The first of its kind, this assembly was of great importance in introducing a new generation of leadership to the ecumenical movement. Soritua Nababan, from Indonesia, became the first youth secretary of the East Asia Christian Conference (EACC), after Epiphania Castro ended her service as the Asian youth secretary of the WCCESSA in 1961. Nababan edited the report of the assembly,[6] containing eight lectures, seven biblical messages and four sermons.

Following the Oslo conference, a youth committee of the New Zealand Council of Churches was formed. Three national Christian youth conferences were held at Blenheim in August 1948, at Palmerston North in

January 1957, and at Lower Hutt, early in 1961. More than 1,300 young people participated in the third conference.[7]

An Australian Christian youth council was created in 1952. It sponsored three Australian conferences of Christian youth (at Mittagong, NSW, January 1952; at Victoria, January 1956; and at Canberra, January 1959). The appointment of full-time youth secretaries in New Zealand and Australia led to a marked increase in ecumenical activity among young people. Many regional and city youth councils were formed and quite a few important consultations were held. Both Australia and New Zealand provided facilities for the training of Asian national youth workers and encouraged a stimulating exchange of leadership within Asia.

Between the inaugural assembly of the EACC at Kuala Lumpur, Malaya, May 1959, and the assembly which met in Bangkok, February-March 1964, its Youth Department had gained considerable ecumenical experience. Four work camp leaders' conferences in Hong Kong, Bangkok, Singapore and Seoul were held, and 90 work camp leaders were trained. They helped to organize 35 international and many national ecumenical work camps. The Youth committee brought 80 youth leaders together in three training institutes and issued various publications. At the EACC assembly in Bangkok, 1964, attention was called "to a tendency in some NCCs to regard their youth secretaries as minor members of staff by not including them in general staff discussions and policy-making or allowing them initiative in other fields". The committee recommended that "youth work should be considered as a movement rather than an institution, that is dynamic and not static in leadership, action and programme".[8] The youth committee was strengthened by five permanent representatives from: (1) India, Pakistan and Ceylon; (2) Burma, Thailand, Malaysia and Vietnam; (3) Indonesia, Philippines; (4) Japan-Okinawa, Korea, China, Taiwan and Hong Kong; (5) Australia and New Zealand. Hiroshi Shinmi from Japan, Levy Griffiths from Australia, and Sang Jung Park from Korea, represented Asia as staff members of the WCC Youth Department in Geneva.

Middle East

In Syria, Lebanon and Egypt there were strong youth movements of the Eastern Orthodox and Coptic churches. The more recently established Protestant churches also had some involvement in youth work. There was remarkable cooperation between the Orthodox and the Evangelicals in both Lebanon and Egypt. The aim of the WCC Youth Department was to foster such cooperation, to give help where it was needed, and to encourage the participation of young members of the Orthodox churches in the ecumenical movement. The first work camp under Orthodox leadership was held in Cyprus. Others were organized in Greece and Lebanon.

A promising development in regional ecumenical conversation was a consultation of Christian youth leaders in Beirut, 18-26 April 1955, sponsored by the World Council of Churches. A year before an ecumenical work camp for the Middle East had been organized in Cyprus. The Beirut gathering was the first ecumenical meeting held in the Middle East after the conference of the International Missionary Council in Jerusalem in 1928. In his opening message, Farid Audeh, chairman of the Near East Christian youth council, stressed that the Middle East faced many problems, in particular the rival philosophies of Islam, Zionism, communism and nationalism competing to shape the future of this region. "If the churches of the Near East are to be active, effective and dynamic in the life of the peoples of this area, and bring to them harmony, love, reconciliation, peace and salvation, they must become *missionary* and *united*." In his address Visser 't Hooft characterized the World Council of Churches "as a first aid station, as a foster mother for Christians whose normal church-mother cannot function, as a postman, as a blood transfusion, as giving substance to the idea of the family of God, as a research laboratory, as a bridge-builder, as a common voice, as a sheepdog, and as a signpost of the *Una Sancta*. A signpost only exists in order to say: go *this* way; don't stand still."

Reports on youth movements in Syria, Lebanon, Jordan, Iran, Iraq, Greece, Cyprus, Egypt and Ethiopia were presented and discussed. William A. Perkins gave an account of his visits to the Middle East and on the successful ecumenical work camp programme in several countries. In the resolutions concern was expressed over "the grave spiritual and material situation of the Arab refugees". Concerning people of different faiths in the Middle East, Christian youth were urged "to witness to their faith through love for their countrymen and the people they live among, by a better understanding of them and what they believe, and by closer spiritual contacts with them".[9] Many of the participants in the Beirut consultation later occupied responsible positions in their respective churches.

In cooperation with the WSCF, the WCC Youth Department established a secretariat for youth and student work in the Middle East with Gabi Habib, a staff member of both the Federation and the Youth Department, as secretary. From 2 to 12 July 1964, an ecumenical youth and student conference of the Middle East was held at Broumana,

Lebanon. Archimandrite George Khodr addressed the gathering on its main theme: "Behold I am making all things new". Nikos Nissiotis spoke on "Our History —a Limitation or Something Creative"; Bishop Karekin Sarkissian on "The Church and the Nation"; Soritua Nababan on "The Churches and the Nations"; René Habashi on "Our New Environment"; and Father Paul Verghese on "The Newness of Our Christian Faith".

Africa

Africa presented a rather different picture. There were few WCC member churches in that continent south of the Sahara, and church youth work was little developed. It should be remembered that Africa (and also the Pacific) were still mission fields and could only be approached through missionary bodies. Membership in the World Council's Youth Department and the nomination of youth delegates to conferences were made by the International Missionary Council.

Ever since 1948, the WCC Youth Department had been urged to send a visitor to West Africa, but the visit took place only in 1953 when the newly appointed chairman, Philip Potter, spent six weeks in Nigeria, the Gold Coast, Angola, Sierra Leone and Liberia. The rapid changes taking place politically and economically were having their effect on the church and its relation to the community. Philip Potter found everywhere an eagerness for a more living relation between young people and the churches.

A youth leaders' training course was held in Nigeria in 1956 under the auspices of the WCCESSA's Youth Department which was supported financially by that department, by world youth projects and the WCC. Another youth planning conference took place at Wilgespruit, South Africa, in May 1957. World youth projects also made possible leadership training courses in Ghana, Gabon, South Africa, and Basutoland. Ecumenical work camps were sponsored in Madagascar, South Africa, the Copperbelt, Northern Rhodesia and the French Congo, with the help of several secretaries for work camps. In 1952, two leaders of the youth movement of the Dutch Reformed Church in South Africa asked the Youth Department of the World Council to help plan for them a six-month tour in Europe and America to study youth work. This was carried through in the second half of 1953.

The All Africa Church Conference at Ibadan, Nigeria, in January 1958 had a section devoted to the consideration of youth work. The situation of youth was described as follows: "Everywhere in Africa young people are poised between two civilizations, between two worlds, unable to see their place clearly and lacking any definite standards of life and thought. As a consequence, they easily develop a materialistic approach to life, or turn idle, leaving their leisure hours unoccupied by useful avocations or any satisfying interests. The growing rate of immorality, particularly in the cities, can be traced to this cause. There is a general thirst for education, which young people make every sacrifice to obtain, but having got it, they do not know how to interpret the Bible in relation to their scientific understanding of the world. Violently drawn into the political preoccupations of their age and country, they frequently find no time for life in the Church... In many places young and old find it difficult to live happily together in the church. Leadership for youth work is hard to come by..."[10]

At the assembly of the All Africa Conference of Churches at Kampala, Uganda, in April 1963, the aims and functions of its youth commission were spelled out as follows: (a) studies and research related to experiences of children and youth; (b) preparation of youth in family, society and church; (c) youth ministry to youth, involvement in prophetic witness and service, experimental approaches; (d) expression of youth and student views with the AACC; (e) ecumenical fellowship and exchange of leaders; (f) recruiting and training of leaders; (g) use of the arts (art, drama, music) in the church.[11]

The youth commission engaged in a series of Bible study meetings and youth leader training institutes. A number of national councils appointed youth secretaries, often financed through world youth projects. The services of Donald Newby, earlier executive director of the Youth Department of the National Council of Churches of Christ in the United States, who served both in Africa and Geneva as a youth secretary for the WCCE, were important to the work of the WCC Youth Department. Bethuel Kiplagat, who led a long-term work camp in Kenya, served the Geneva staff as associate secretary for several years for Ecumenical Youth Service.

The first All Africa Christian Youth Assembly was held at Nairobi, December 1962-January 1963, under the sponsorship of all the organizations represented in the World Christian Youth Commission. Three hundred and eighty young people from 35 African countries met around the theme "Freedom under the Cross", and explored how they could participate actively in the renewal and life of the church. Adeolu Adegbola was the organizing secretary. Eight Bible studies on the Acts of the Apostles were given by W.H. Crane, Africa secretary of the WSCF. Among the speakers were Richard Andriamanjato, Brigalia Bam, Bola Ige, John Karefa-Smart, J.G. Kiano, Bethuel Kiplagat, Jean Kotto, James Lawson, John Mpaye, Henry Okullu and Paul Verghese. In the assembly message it was stressed that "the structures of the churches and patterns of worship should respond to the needs of the present time and reflect the aspirations of the African personality".

North America

The United Christian Youth Movement in America, officially established in 1934 when the Christian youth council of North America met at Lake Geneva, Wisconsin, was already a strong and well-organized interchurch body keen to establish ecumenical relations with the rest of the world. In 1944, 800 youth delegates from all parts of the United States and Canada gathered at Lakeside, Ohio, to receive inspiration and to make plans for the task of reconstructing a war-torn world. As far back as 1945 a youth secretary was appointed and attached to the New York office of the World Council of Churches. The Youth Department owed much to the enthusiasm and energy of the young people in the United States. Both the work camp programme and the world youth projects had their origin in the USA. The WCC Youth Department, in its turn, has given to Christian youth in North America the opportunity to work in close cooperation with young Christians from the rest of the world.

After a few special consultations with youth workers and leaders in both Canada and the United States on "The Integration of Youth in the Life and Mission of the Church", the office in New York was closed in November 1957. The youth department of the National Council of Churches of Christ, which was made up of representative youth workers of churches in the USA, now took a more direct responsibility for ecumenical youth work.

From the 1930s there had been large interdenominational youth conferences in North America. The last of these was convened in 1952. In the style of earlier cooperative American Christian movements, these conferences were open to all interested young people from local youth groups and to leaders of national church youth movements. After 1952, the denominational youth departments wanted a new form of ecumenical youth meeting to be developed. The North American ecumenical youth assembly on the campus of the University of Michigan, at Ann Arbor, from 16 to 23 August 1961, was truly a product of the churches which had all along taken a lead in ecumenical affairs in North America. The assembly was prepared over a period of three years by a committee representing chiefly the "mainline" Protestant churches, convened by the youth department of the NCCUSA and the committee on young people's work of the Canadian Council of Churches acting together with the WCC and the WCCESSA.

It was a gathering of Christian "youth" and not of university students. Represented were the International Society of Christian Endeavour, Boy Scouts of America, Girl Scouts of the USA, Campfire Girls, the YMCA, the YWCA and the Ministry to Armed Forces Personnel. There were some 1,850 young people and youth leaders representing almost forty US and Canadian denominations as well as nearly forty countries outside North America. The federated Russian Orthodox youth clubs and the Greek Orthodox youth of America sent small delegations.

The programme of the assembly was built around the main theme "Entrusted with the Message of Reconciliation" and developed the sub-themes "The World We Live In", "The Gospel We Live Under", and "The Mission of the Church". Among the speakers were George Johnston of the United Theological College of McGill University in Montreal, and U Kyaw Than, associate general secretary of the East Asia Christian Conference. Robert Seaver of Union Theological Seminary in New York directed the dramatic productions. In his evaluation of the Ann Arbor assembly, Roderick French noted "that 'the world' as the contemporary world-wide arena of mankind was somewhat neglected", in spite of the fact that at last some people were ready "to do some necessary and careful thinking about the relation of Christianity and culture". He added that "the closing address of William Stringfellow reasserted the very concrete world in which our fellow men pass their daily lives, but that came as a parting reminder of something too much overlooked in the preceding days".[12]

The Ann Arbor assembly opened a new period in ecumenical youth work in North America, as the Lausanne assembly did in Europe. Denominational youth departments and individual delegates were forced to spell out the implications of what took place on the campus of the Michigan University. Philip Potter's words in his letter of greetings became a challenge to many participants: "The theme of the Assembly, 'Entrusted with the Message of Reconciliation', is more significant today than when it was first chosen. More than ever the forces of division in our world are virulently active, and North America, both within the continent and in its relations with the rest of the world, finds itself in the middle of these forces of division."[13]

Latin America

The world survey of youth work in the churches from 1948 to 1950 had discovered in Argentina, Brazil, Chile, Colombia, Cuba, Mexico, Puerto Rico, Peru and Uruguay national federations of young people, working together in the Union of Evangelical Youth of Latin America (ULAJE), under the auspices of which regional conferences had been held with conspicuous success in 1941 and 1946. ULAJE was formed on the initiative of Latin American youth leaders who had attended the first world youth conference in Amsterdam in 1939. The churches in several Latin American nations were developing an ecumenical outlook. The approach of the WCC Youth Department and of the WCCE was welcomed by young people of these areas. An almost immediate result was the development of an active relationship with Christian youth work, especially in parts of Europe.

The congress of ULAJE at Rio de Janeiro, held in December 1951, put its main emphasis on evangelism and ecumenism. Wilmina Rowland, secretary of youth work of the WCCE, and William Keys, secretary in New York of the WCC Youth Department, attended this meeting.

An ecumenical team of six youth leaders representing Canada, France, Sweden, the United States and India, under the leadership of B. Molander, visited Mexico, Costa Rica, Colombia, Ecuador, Peru, Bolivia, Chile, Argentina, Uruguay, Paraguay, Brazil, Venezuela and Cuba from December 1956 to February 1957, and participated in the fourth congress of ULAJE in Barranquilla, Colombia, in December. The main purpose of the visitation was to interpret the ecumenical movement to Christian youth in Latin America, to share with them the concerns and experiences of Christian youth in other parts of the world, and to survey the needs of youth work in the area.

Bengt-Thure Molander, reporting on the ecumenical team visit and his own individual visits to Latin America, made the following observations: "Latin American Protestantism is now more and more nationally rooted. It is evangelistic in its essence, individualistic in the positive and negative sense, moralistic in attitude, and emotionally strong. It is anti-ecumenical, but, with a new generation which is open to theological influences from abroad, is already contributing to a new understanding of the mission of the church in an area of rapid social change, and is rediscovering what the church really is."[14]

In the late fifties and early sixties ULAJE cooperated closely with the WCC/WCCE Youth Departments, with the youth and student committee on cooperation in Latin America, the WSCF and other international and national ecumenical youth movements. Its new secretary, Oscar Bolioli, served as vice-chairman of the committee on the WCC Youth Department, thus ensuring continual contact between Geneva and Montevideo. Regional secretaries were appointed in the Rio de la Plata area, the Caribbean and Brazil. The youth departments of Argentina and Brazil developed their annual institutes. A series of publications was brought out. A number of work camps were conducted in countries such as Bolivia, Brazil, Paraguay, and Costa Rica, and several youth leaders' training courses were organized, such as a course in Costa Rica for the Central American and Caribbean countries in 1960, in which some 40 young people from 12 countries participated. A similar youth leaders' course was organized in Brazil in 1961. The WCC Youth Department published in October 1963 a whole number of *Youth* on regional developments and the question of indigenization. Its chief burden was that the ecumenical movement should serve to bring regional experience and commitment into a universal dialogue.

NOTES

[1] *The First Assembly of the World Council of Churches,* Amsterdam, 22 August-4 September 1948, ed. W.A. Visser 't Hooft, London, SCM Press, 1949, p.62.

[2] *The Ecumenical Review*, Vol. IV, No. 2, January 1952, p.163.

[3] "Youth in Asia", Vol. II, No. 3, 1950, pp.259-66.

[4] *Looking Ahead in Christian Youth Work*, reports of recent consultations, Bangalore and Allahabad, Nagpur, National Christian Council, 1953.

[5] *News Sheet*, Youth Department, No. 3, 1957, pp.23-24.

[6] *Christ the Life*, Colombo, 1965.

[7] *One Lord, One World,* report of the Third Ecumenical Youth Conference, Lower Hutt, 27 December 1960-4 January 1961, Christchurch, YCNCC, 1961, p.63.

[8] Bangkok, 25 February-5 March 1964, *Minutes* (Part One), Bangkok, 1964, pp.47-48.

[9] Report, Geneva, WCC Youth Department, 1955, pp.73, 13-14, 64.

[10] *The Church in Changing Africa*, New York, International Missionary Council, 1958, p.30.

[11] *Drumbeats from Kampala*, London, Lutterworth Press, 1963, pp.74-75.

[12] "The Assembly in Ecumenical Perspective", *Youth*, No. 4, November 1961, pp.19-20.

[13] *Ibid.*, p.22.

[14] *News Sheet*, Youth Department, No. 2, 1957, p.22.

VI. New Delhi 1961
to Uppsala 1968

During these seven years the major function of the Youth Deparment of the World Council of Churches was that of liaisoning between the younger generation of Christians and the leadership of the ecumenical movement. As young people became increasingly vocal in the movement, the churches had to take seriously their contributions in their constituencies. Young ecumenists became active both in making statements of principles and in experimental actions. Often many of their activities were not looked upon with favour by church leaders. Tension, and sometimes even conflict between generations, became an ecumenical reality. The Youth Department made a great effort to interpret what was actually happening among young people to the older churchmen and women and to prevent the unnecessary alienation that frequently resulted from misunderstanding.

The young people of this period were much less interested in churchly ecumenism — the attempt to involve denominations in the ecumenical movement — than in common action on the local scene involving groups from different confessions. This interest was partly the consequence of an exciting discovery of unity among those who longed for the renewal of the life of the church; it was also due to their disappointment with the institutional inertia of the churches. The common search for an honest expression of faith and a viable structure for the Christian community in the world held for them more reality than the effort to reconcile divided traditions or the disagreements over expressions of doctrinal truths and the structures of the church.

Christian youth in the sixties lost much of the interest in conferences and study programmes, not because they disregarded the necessity of encounter and study, but because they saw that the findings of such meetings were rarely implemented in the life of the churches. They were inclined to pay greater heed to what had been said in the past and to act on it. In the assemblies and conferences of the World Council they pushed

Above: First World Conference of Christian Youth, Amsterdam 1939 (Photo: Pers-Foto-Bureau "H.E.N.O.")

Left: From left to right, Philip A. Potter, Jean Fraser and Roderick French (Photo: WCC)

Below: Third World Conference of Christian Youth, Travancore 1952 (Photo: WCC)

*Left: Conference on
"Faith, Science and the Future",
Boston 1979
(Photo: WCC)*

*Below: Consultation on humanity
and wholeness of persons with
disabilities, Sao Paulo, 1981
(Photo: Nair Benedicto)*

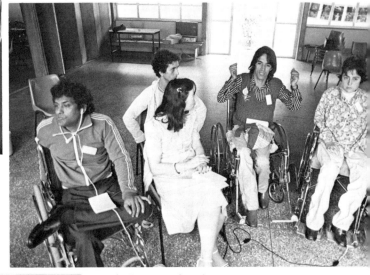

*Left: Ecumenical work camp
(Photo: WCC/John Fulton)*

*Below: A volunteer bus driver
reads* Hot News *at Uppsala, 1968
(Photo: WCC)*

for action. They wanted action and reflection to be intimately woven together. Christian education and theology were not seen as a preparation for life, but as a commentary on it, written from the perspective of involvement. The voice of authority, whether it criticized or endorsed their actions, was only heard and accepted when it spoke from within the struggle for an authentic Christian presence in the world.

In contrast to the period between Evanston and New Delhi during which some emphasis was placed on the teenager, the focal point after New Delhi became the young adult. Developments within the ecumenical movement since the Second Vatican Council and the preparations for the world conference on Church and Society in 1966 had an impact on the content of the programme of the Youth Department. The concern for the integration of youth in the life of the church gave way to the concern for the contribution of the younger generation to the missionary structures of the church. The successful series of regional ecumenical youth assemblies produced an intensified demand for regional youth organizations and brought back the demand for a new world conference of Christian youth. But the Youth Department participated in and stimulated other meetings, and was not too eager to organize its own conferences. Some regional ecumenical youth assemblies in Africa, Latin America, the Middle East and Asia were co-sponsored, usually in close cooperation with the other organizations in the World Christian Youth Commission.

One hundred and sixty young people met for a week in New Delhi in 1961 to prepare for the fullest possible participation in the WCC assembly in their several roles as youth delegates, stewards and aids. There were orientation sessions on the life and work of the World Council over the past seven years, with special reference to the task of "this generation", and the young people were given a picture of the church in Asia, its present situation and future challenges. They considered the assembly theme and related themes in terms of the role of young people. Several sessions were devoted to the concerns of the Youth Department and the contributions the youth participants could make to the Assembly. They were probably the best prepared of all who came to New Delhi, both eager and enthusiastic to implement a vision. Visser 't Hooft challenged them "to work, pray and sweat" for the cause of Christian unity at all levels. But they soon discovered that above all they were called also to patience and understanding as they were confronted with the slowness of their elders and their churches.

Philip Potter warned: "We are in serious danger of driving young people to despair of the churches and therefore in flight from them" and the work of the church "may perish for lack of younger men and women to take it up, because they despair of anything really happening in it". Evidence of this despair was particularly manifested in the question of intercommunion, on which Philip Potter said: "Intercommunion is the deepest inner reality of the People of God without which they cannot truly render a common witness to the world."[1] Even though the plea of youth that "one baptism must lead us to one table" was discussed by the Committee on Faith and Order, no definite proposal came before the Assembly.

An issue of *Youth* was devoted to the problem of "Many Churches, One Table, One Church" with contributions by Keith R. Bridston, Roderick French, Albert van den Heuvel, Johannes Hoekendijk, N.G. Nissiotis and John A.T. Robinson. At the end the recommendations for services of holy communion at ecumenical gatherings of Bossey 1961 and Lund 1952 were reprinted in parallel columns. Hoekendijk emphasized in particular the eschatological dimension of the sacrament of communion: "Communion as an eschatalogical sacrament is the representation of the Kingdom in the *world*; it is impossible to lock up the Kingdom in the church... Intercommunion is not a question between denominations but between nations, not of intercommunion between all sorts of confessions but between people of all sorts. Communion is the first fulfilment of the 'feast that the Lord will make for all nations' (Isa. 25:6)."[2]

"Youth in a Complex Society" was the theme of a consultation at Zeist, Holland, 12-16 October 1964. An attempt was made to define terms like secularization, secularism and identification. There was wide agreement that "*kenosis* (self-emptying) of itself may achieve nothing; *kenosis* must be directed to an end; in the context of Philippians 2 *kenosis* was for the sake of unity; in the context of today *kenosis* of the church must also be directed towards unity, of world and church, that both may be at one in God".[3]

Hoekendijk contributed a penetrating analysis of the meaning of mission in modern complex situations. He pointed out that for centuries mission had been "the fatal reduction of the apostolate into a more or less peripheral affair".[4] Hoekendijk asserted that we must devise missionary structures inductively, close and relevant to the human situation, refrain from the customary mental movement from the ministry to the laity, attempt to synchronize the church's calendar with the various secular calendars, and be content with ad hoc, temporary structures.

It was not accidental that at the world conference on Church and Society in Geneva, July 1966, considerable attention was devoted in Section IV to the tensions between the generations: "Man and Community in Changing Societies". These tensions were considered normal and probably permanent. For the first time, a common understanding of history is no more shared. Discontinuity of experience is caused by the rapid and revolutionary changes in technology and in the social order, in particular through migration and the urbanization of youth. The schools which train the young are outside the control of the parents. As birth control devices are fast removing the risk of accidental conception, the traditional value system has to reckon with a whole new situation. Another illustration of the tension between generations may be found in their attitudes to war. "Adults usually declare war and send their young people to fight it." The vocation of the adolescent is now to establish his or her identity, to explore the future and to choose a direction. "Guidance which suggests the slightest manipulation alienates (them) very quickly." In the church and the community at large authority which is taken for granted is severely questioned. "This is not to say that authority as such is rejected; on the contrary, young people seem to be constantly searching for it."[5]

Several consultations were held on other specific topics. Two meetings on "Confessionalism and the Ecumenical Movement" took place at Rochester, USA, 17-22 August 1963, and at Geneva, 2-5 October 1963. The question was raised as to whether "confessionalistic thought is not prone to look backwards in its theology, and thus is in danger of failing to meet the challenges of the present time... No church today can feel absolutely sure of itself and absolutely self-satisfied if it merely asks what is its own understanding of itself. It must also be prepared to let others question it." The consultations reached the conclusion that "the ecumenical movement and the confession must not and cannot be opposed to one another. Those who want the ecumenical movement without any clear confession are missing the church's witness to the world. Those whose confession does not recognize faith in the unity of the church are missing the message of the gospel." Replies sent in from the World Alliance of Reformed Churches, the World Convention of Churches of Christ (Disciples), and the International Congregational Council confirmed this statement. It was recommended that young participants in ecumenical gatherings should be far better prepared "to know the living signs of renewal, the attempts to restate the faith, and the experiments at wholeness and obedience which have been tried out in their church during recent years".

"Confessional Loyalty at all Costs?" was the title of *Risk* No. 4, 1966 (since 1965 *Risk* was the new serial publication of the Youth Department). Outlining the contents of this issue, Albert H. van den Heuvel wrote that youth feels strongly that confessional youth conferences in an ecumenical age are outdated and wrong. They cannot but pray that their denominations may disappear into united forms of church life. Youth needs a minimum confession in order to manifest its maximum commitment. World confessional bodies should tell Christians about local ecumenical experiments in which their churches are involved. The real battle is fought at the local level where the cost and the possibilities of really daring action become apparent. The role of the world confessional organizations has changed since their member churches covenanted together in the ecumenical movement.

After more than three years of preparation, a dialogue between younger members of the Western and Orthodox traditions on youth in rapid social change took place at Thessalonica, 5-11 September 1965. Evaluating this conference with its theme "Youth in the Modern World", Albert van den Heuvel made several observations on some major tensions between the two groups. "A passionate plea was made by the Western delegation for a dialogue between church and the world, in which the world would write the agenda and the church would be ready to commit itself humbly to giving contributions in all fields of life. Many Orthodox and some of the Protestants were shocked by the vehemence of this plea. They did not like the way in which church and world were separated and even made into opposites...".6

The International Christian Youth Exchange (ICYE), the WSCF's section involved in the European SCM school movements and the European working group of the WCC Youth Department together sponsored a meeting with youth in Duisburg, Germany, during the first week of August 1967, around the theme: "Revolution: the Struggle for True Humanity". Out of the 183 participants, 115 were students who had spent a year overseas, sponsored by ICYE. The consultation questioned present systems of education, which cater to the individual for his or her own self-advancement. They were critical of the heavy academic subject discipline of schools which tends to ignore the dimensions of social change in a world of economic and political injustice, and they questioned the adequacy of present nation-centred school systems.

A short description of the International Christian Youth Exchange may not be out of place here. The first exchanges were organized by the Church of the Brethren from Germany to the USA in 1949. In 1957 ICYE was formally created by five denominations in the United States as an independent church-sponsored agency. Two years later a first meeting of representatives of the European ICYE committees took place. In 1966 the international committee of ICYE was created to give more organizational reality to what had been a process of informal consultation. This committee supervised the worldwide programme which at that stage included some countries in Asia and Latin America, and also the first exchanges between countries within Europe and between Europe and Asia. The programme was designed for young people of 16-18 years of age. The International Council for ICYE was formed legally in 1969, and began operating the following year with headquarters in Geneva. In 1977 the International Council was dissolved and the new federation formed. New headquarters were established in Berlin.

In the 1950s there was a strong emphasis on the church and Christian commitment in the programme. It was a time of church growth, increased church attendance and active youth organizations in the churches. Developments in the 1960s were quite different. Religious commitment did not weaken, but it was interpreted in different ways. In the annual consultations and in the international committee vigorous discussions on how to understand the aims and purposes of ICYE took place. It became increasingly conscious of the fact that in the United States and in Europe especially the decade was marked by turmoil, protest by youth students, and the demand for international economic justice. There was, moreover, the sexual revolution and the experience of liberation from traditional ideas and patterns of behaviour in different areas of life.

During the 1970s ICYE faced a financial crisis. The separation of the US programme from the international operation brought to light the precarious position of the programme. Furthermore, the nature of international exchange was called in question. Was it a programme *for* youth or a movement *of* youth? The Woodstock generation challenged the foundations of ICYE. At the international committee meeting in Berlin in 1969 it was spelled out that "ICYE seeks to enable all participants to discover the common bonds they share with the whole of humanity. ICYE therefore seeks encounter with persons of all convictions and invites participation of those who share its aims and who wish to take part in its programmes." In spite of the difficulties it faced, ICYE remained a part of the ecumenical movement and supports the recent aim of the World Council of Churches in the realm of "ecumenical sharing of resources". From its beginning until recently over 10,000 young people from more than 40 countries have participated in this exchange programme. This meant that over 30,000 persons were touched and changed by the programme, as hosts or co-workers. William Perkins, who was the ICYE Director from 1958 to 1972, wrote an extensive article on the history of ICYE in *International Newsletter*.[7]

During the period from New Delhi to Uppsala, the Youth Department held several other annual consultations of ecumenical youth secretaries in Europe which discussed the various activities of the Department, relations to youth networks, regional conferences, cooperation with the All Christian Peace Assembly in Prague, the Conference of European Churches, the Kirchentag in Germany and the International Christian Youth Exchange. The meeting at Radevormwald in Rhineland, 14-16 October 1961, was for the first time attended by some representatives of Roman Catholic youth. The annual meeting at Josefstal, near Munich, 7-11 October 1963, concentrated on a theological reflection on evangelism and the missionary structure of the congregation.

During the 17th autumn consultation at Koppelsberg, near Plön/ Holstein, 14-21 October 1966, the theme was "International Economic Justice". The consultation was enriched by the presence of delegates and staff of the world conference on Church and Society, held in the summer of 1966 in Geneva. At the meeting of European correspondents in Wiener-Neustadt, Austria, 9-14 October 1967, the debate on international economic justice was continued. A whole number of *Risk*, "The Development Apocalypse, or Will International Justice Kill the Ecumenical Movement?", was published in the spring of 1967. As some forty million people die of starvation each year, the word "apocalypse" was used to indicate the "not-so-gradual movement towards chaos and misery such as the world has never known".

Reinhold von Thadden-Trieglaff, a leader among Christian students and in the Confessing Church in Germany, and his friends started the experiment of the German Kirchentag in 1949. As they took advantage of the new opportunity for engaging in public activities offered to the church, which had been subjected to persecution for so long, they were determined to proclaim "the blessing of a new start". They planned to do this by confronting church people with secular experts and administrators, and by reinterpreting the gospel in terms of the present situation and the future tasks. Not only did the Kirchentag become the only important meeting place for German people from both East and West Germany; it soon developed into a truly international ecumenical event. Roman Catholic participation in it grew rapidly through the years.

The massive efficiency and success of the Kirchentag attracted in the sixties many of the younger generation, and they looked on the Kirchentag as a place where burning questions of conviction and commitment could be discussed in open court, and brought to the public mind through major secular newspapers, radio and television channels. Bible study was combined with the discussion of the current problems of modern life. The small groups into which the Kirchentag had been divided, and the regional and local meetings which had prepared for its great rallies, had given many lay and young people an experience of personal participation in Christian thinking, and encouraged them to speak their own minds. The WCC Youth Department and its constituency played an active role in the Kirchentag in Munich (1959), Berlin (1961), Dortmund (1963), Cologne (1965), Hannover (1967). Many young people from abroad, not included in the quotas of the special youth delegation, attended the various Kirchentag rallies, all wrestling with problems of justice, peace and development and asking how a supernatural concept of God and the postulate of divine action in creation can go with an understanding of the rational responsibility of humankind.

The Christian Peace Conference (CPC) held its first Assembly in Prague in 1958. It originated in the desire of Protestant Christians in Eastern Europe to find in the conditions of their socialist countries a way in which Christians might address themselves to world affairs as Christians and not merely as loyal citizens of their countries. The moving spirit of the CPC was Josef L. Hromadka of the Comenius Theological Faculty in Prague. In 1960 a section of young people, called "the young CPC" was integrated into the larger body of the conference as one of its standing commissions. From 1960 to 1968 the chairman of the Youth Commission was Milan Opocensky. It was in the beginning a rather docile organ. At the second assembly in 1964 the youth group, however, formulated a statement that a theology of revolution was necessary but that this would have to be preceded by a revolution in theology. The youth commission dealt with the themes of revolution and status quo, oppressive structures, bureaucratic institutions, and sloganistic thinking. It observed "that even the CPC, which was intended to be an open and free-minded movement, was becoming a rigid and bureaucratic organization. Certain questions and concerns were ruled out of order if, in the eyes of some, they posed a threat to organizational stability and respectability".[8] The youth commission was branded as Maoist for mentioning China in its resolutions, and for its questioning of the static concept of peaceful coexistence.

The WCC Youth Department gave its support to an international Christian seminar for young people in Prague, 21 August-2 September 1965, jointly organized by the Christian Peace Conference and the Friends Service Council in London. The meeting stressed that it is essential to distinguish between real and false revolution and between real and false peace efforts. After its annual commission meeting in West Berlin in 1967 the latent tension between the Youth Commission and the CPC itself came out into the open and a confrontation became unavoidable. The international secretariat rejected the report of the West Berlin meeting, asked for a censure of the youth commission and refused to publish the report. At the meeting of the working committee in Zagorsk in

July 1967, Josef Hromadka defended the position of the Youth Commission and said that if he were a member of it he would resign from the CPC rather than be treated in such a way. His opinion was shared by few others in the inner organs of the CPC.

The events of August 1968 drove Hromadka into direct opposition with those with whom he had so long laboured for peace and social justice. In his public letter condemning the Warsaw Pact occupation of his country he said: "My basic feeling is that of disappointment, regret and shame. In my long life, I do not know of a greater tragedy." The response of his cherished Christian Peace Conference was even more tragic, as those committed to the status quo and opportunism undermined the authority of the Czech leader within the CPC and actively organized an opposition party, as it were, which would perform according to the dictates of partisan politics rather than in dedication to peace and social justice. Hromadka offered his resignation in November 1969. He died six months later.[9]

The first assembly of the Conference of European Churches at Nyborg, Denmark, in 1959 was concerned with youth work, besides being interested in issues like evangelism, social and political responsibility, interchurch aid, and the active participation of the Orthodox churches. Albert H. van den Heuvel represented the Youth Department at the second assembly in Nyborg in October 1960 and at the third assembly in October 1962 at which group 4 discussed the theme: "Responsible Cooperation between Different Generations". The theme of the fourth Nyborg assembly was: "Living together as Continents and Generations". A youth delegation of fifteen members, appointed by the European youth working group, was present at this gathering. W. Gorzewski, the work camps secretary, served as the convener of the youth delegation. At the joint meeting of the presidium and advisory committee of the CEC in Vienna, in February 1965, it was resolved that its secretary be authorized to have official contacts with the European national youth correspondents group with a view to discussing possible arrangements for a closer and more formal collaboration.

The WCC Youth Department submitted to the fifth assembly at Nyborg in October 1967 an extensive report on international economic justice in which the global picture, the urgency of the situation, a new direction and the involvement of the church were outlined. The report recommended that the CEC take up the issues of development as a first priority and invite experts from the southern nations to participate actively in the deliberations. The 45 youth delegates to the 1967 assembly had a voice but not a vote unless they were part of the official delegation of their churches. At the meeting of the presidium in Ravello near Naples, October 1968, the European working group of the WCC was divided in its opinion about the relationship with the CEC. A majority was in favour of closer cooperation between the future Ecumenical Youth Council in Europe (EYCE) and the CEC. A minority preferred to see the Youth Council act as an independent body. It was decided at the first meeting of the executive committee of the Ecumenical Youth Council in Leuenberg, Switzerland, October 1968, that it needed through the CEC close programmatic and financial relationships with youth movements, also because the CEC had not been actively engaged in youth work.

Although 17,000 young people discovered the ecumenical movement through personal involvement in ecumenical work camps between 1948 and 1968, the Youth Department increasingly became aware of the limitations of work camps. There were many human needs which called for kinds of services other than pick-and-shovel work. Refugees, migrant workers, disabled children, and marginalized and forgotten people in the backyards of societies demanded social service projects in which young people could express their responsibility and concern in a more relevant and direct way. The Youth Department's programme started, therefore, to include, besides construction or restoration projects, community service work. The name was consequently changed from ecumenical work camps to ecumenical youth service to indicate the wider range of possibilities for active engagement and service.

In view of the demands for voluntary service in developing nations and of the willingness of young people to volunteer for longer periods, the Youth Department began to sponsor from 1962 onwards long-term ecumenical work camps, lasting for ten months. These increased the effectiveness of the service rendered and the extent of the ecumenical encounter among the volunteers and between them and the local church and people. Long-term projects were carried out in Kenya, Thailand, Indonesia and Korea. The services of C.I. Itty from an Asian-Orthodox background enriched the activities of the Youth Department.

Alongside the discussions and studies raised within the discussion of international economic justice, the staff and the national and regional youth service committees continued to re-evaluate the programme in the light of new insights and developments in order to find the best possible diaconal tasks for young people. Through annual leadership orientation courses and consultations of national correspondents in Europe, through leadership training courses and study conferences in the Congo (1964), in Japan and Zambia (1965), in Lebanon (1966), through participation in conferences and consultations of the Coordinating Committee for International Voluntary Service (affiliated with UNESCO) in Hungary (1963), Austria (1964), Poland (1965), Argentina (1966), and through close contact with the officers for the Young World Mobilization Appeal for the Freedom from Hunger Campaign by the Food and Agriculture Organization, the Department attempted to find the most relevant and effective forms of ecumenical youth service.

By varying the size of the teams from five to thirty participants and the periods of service from four to six weeks, or even to ten months, and above all, by trying to set up projects answering the most urgent needs of various societies, the Youth Department was able to find a means by which young people could make a genuine contribution to nation-building and to the renewal of the church. Six hundred youth service projects provided a taste of unity for several thousands of young people in small, international, inter-racial and interconfessional communities, and so contributed in a very practical and down-to-earth manner to the ecumenical movement.

World youth projects continued as a joint programme of the WCC Youth Department and the WCCE. It was administered by the joint youth committee of these two bodies with the help of youth secretaries from the different regions. The programme sought to develop and strengthen youth work around the world through an exchange of funds, ideas, personnel and written material. It was a means of equipping regional and national youth secretaries with resources to develop strategies for their areas, in ways relevant to their situations. Churches increasingly took responsibility for experiments for renewal among youth in the ecumenical movement in other countries.

The amount for a project ranged from $500 to $4,200. Since 1964, world youth projects were included in the service programme and list of projects of the WCC Division of Inter-Church Aid, Refugee and World Service. As a result, there was, in some nations, an increasing coordination between the national and interchurch aid agency and the ecumenical youth council in securing support for projects related to ecumenical youth work. Soon projects were listed for no more than three to five years with the expectation that, at the end of the period, they would become self-supporting. Support for the programme came in a number of ways. National interchurch aid agencies in which youth was involved in the raising of funds were contributing considerable amounts. Help from national denominations was on the increase as well. An interesting feature was the small but significant growth of support from Africa and Asia for projects in this programme in their own and other continents.

Especially in its growing contacts with Roman Catholic youth work, the Youth Department was confronted with the need for "vertical youth work", dealing with such problems as youth in industry, rural youth and unattached youth. The Youth Department had, however, more frequent contacts with the Roman Catholic agricultural youth organization (MIJARC), because both organizations had a staff member at the Food and Agriculture Organization headquarters. The Youth Departments of the WCC and the WCCE, the WSCF, and the World YMCA and YWCA sponsored a consultation on "Unattached Youth" at Annecy, France, 1-6 April 1967, in which Roman Catholics participated. Accounts were given of work among youth in Amsterdam, Berlin, Birmingham, Glasgow, London and Paris. The term "unattached" was used to refer to those young people whose needs are not met by any type of organized activity. The report of this consultation was widely distributed. The hope was expressed that particularly after the Uppsala Assembly Protestants and Roman Catholics would combine their efforts in parish youth work and in specialized youth ministries, especially since the development issue had become such an important one.

Reference has been made in this chapter to certain issues of *Risk*. Its circulation doubled in these years and some issues, such as "Ministry of Meanings" and "New Hymns for a New Day" reached a circulation of more than 10,000. Stephen C. Rose, editor of *Renewal Magazine*, joined the Youth Department as staff writer for a period during 1966-67 and carried major responsibility for several issues. The publication of a worship booklet, *Congregemur*,[10] in three languages followed the appearance of a handbook for youth leaders, *New Creation and New Generation*.[11] The handbook remains one of the finest collections of essays on youth work from theological, sociological, psychological, and historical perspectives, with contributions from Roderick S. French, Ross Snyder, Albert H. van den Heuvel, C.I. Itty, John Paul Frelick and Samuel Amsler.

"Youth in God's World" remains undoubtedly one of the most search-ing documents which the WCC Youth Department has ever produced. In preparation for Uppsala 1968 it was included in the work book for the Assembly Committees.[12] In the twenty years of its existence the Youth Department had never before written a position paper on youth in God's world. The first draft of this first paper was sent to 500 youth workers around the world. Their comments and the deliberations of the WCC/WCCE youth committee led in 1965 to a second draft which was then again sent around the world to those who had sent in comments. The third draft was again scrutinized by the same committee before the paper was finalized. The document honestly admitted in the introduction that "youth can experiment courageously and dangerously with traditions and reject inherited value systems. The search for security can make them also ruthlessly egocentric and conservative."[13]

Youth lives with hands stretched out towards the future, be it with cheap expectations of easily acquired luxury or with a deep commitment to a more human life for themselves and others. It is not youth which is the hope of the future, but the future which is the hope of youth. An allegiance to renewal as the implementation of hope is the only real antidote for the problems of the younger generation. It was noted that "only a small percentage of the younger generation is organized in programmes which the adult society offers to them, and most of them complain that while they really want to care, they are cared for". The document concentrated on the age group 16-25, although its contributors were aware of the fact that age represents different characteristics in different societies and that terms such as teenager, young adult, adolescent, youth, young person have different connotations in different cultures.

With regard to the tension between generations the following observations were made: "The Western culture exalts tension as necessary for personal development and structural change. Eastern culture tends rather to stress its fears of conflict. In each approach an essential element of the picture is shown. Translating the destructive conflict between the generations into a productive tension is not an easy thing. Education of adults is probably as much needed as education for young people. But we are convinced that the problem needs more than education.... Many young people distrust basically all education and youth work methods because they seem not to allow young people to find identity and responsibility but rather present them with an unreal choice, to accept or to stay out, to conform or to rebel.... Only when young and old will accept the challenge of a common future together and build their lives into service will the conflict disappear and the tension become productive.... Separate youth work, which does not aim at a reconciliation of the generations and does not make this aim visible in its activities, does not belong to the church."[14]

The last sentence should not be interpreted in a churchly sense. The paper made it quite clear that youth work should be mainly organized in a secular way. The churches should offer services to young people — space to meet, a chance to be together with the older generation — "whether this brings to, or keeps young people in the church or not". There was also a strong warning in the document against the idolizing of youth

80   *From Generation to Generation*

which appears like a new form of paternalism. Enthusiastic applause for protest is as harmful as authoritarian refusal to identify its causes.

In the conclusion it was stated: "...A youth ministry should... never become a nervous effort to keep young people in or win them for the church. A style of life which is inspired by the gospel and a genuine care for a new generation is all that is required. The message of good news is strong enough to excite, engage and commit those of all ages".[15]

NOTES

[1] "Going Forward Together Into Manifest Unity", *The Ecumenical Review*, Vol. XIV, No. 3, April 1962, pp.345 and 347.
[2] "Exceptions, Eschatology and Our Common Practices", *Youth*, December 1962, p.75.
[3] *Youth*, No. 10, November 1964, p.113.
[4] *Ibid.*, pp.138-145.
[5] *World Conference on Church and Society*, Geneva, 12-26 July 1966, report, Geneva, WCC, 1967, pp.170-174.
[6] Youth archives, Europe.
[7] No. 2, July 1983, pp.3-11.
[8] *1960-1970: Documents of the Youth Commission of the Christian Peace Conference*, eds Brewster Kneen and Cathie Kneen, 1971, mimeographed, p.2.
[9] *Ibid.*, p.3.
[10] "Let Us Come Together", a worship booklet for modern young people, Geneva, WCC, 1965, rev. 1967.
[11] A forum for youth workers, ed. Albert H. van den Heuvel, New York, Friendship Press, 1965.
[12] *Work Book for the Assembly Committees*, Uppsala, 1968, Geneva, WCC, 1968, pp.137-152. See also *Risk*, Vol. IV, No. 3, 1968.
[13] *Ibid.*, p.138.
[14] *Ibid.*, pp.141, 140, 149.
[15] *Ibid.*, p.152.

VII. Uppsala 1968
to Nairobi 1975

An All European Seminar was held in East Berlin, 22-26 April 1968, in preparation for the Fourth Assembly of the World Council of Churches in Uppsala, Sweden. The meeting concentrated in particular on Section VI of the Assembly: "Towards New Styles of Living". It submitted six proposals concerning greater personal sacrifices in time, thought and money, new life-styles in one's own communities, a more universal education, greater involvement in the changing of oppressive political structures, an open-mindedness continually questioning the information flow. The statement ended with the words: "Church structure is dead; long live movement! Let us all take part in the Lord's Supper in Uppsala."

A long list of the ways to voice the strong concerns of youth at Uppsala was drawn up at the Berlin seminar. All youth participants should adopt one or two delegates as special targets for pressure. They should use common means of demonstrations in the forms of sit-in, stand-up, walk-out, laugh-out, picketing, sit-down, boycott. Youth should create influen-tial relations with the press and television. It should use large banners inside and outside the assembly hall and air its views on posters, in buses, dining rooms, toilets, and on badges. Material should be distributed to delegates in their private rooms. Each day there should be a teaching event to sharpen the discussion of crucial issues.

A total of 127 young people of 18 to 30 years of age gathered in Uppsala 1-3 July 1968, for a preparatory conference dealing with the theme and sub-themes of the Fourth Assembly. They were the official youth delegates invited by the WCC Executive Committee to attend the assembly and to participate in its activities, with the right to speak with the chairman's permission but not to vote. One-half of the delegates came from the third world and a significant number were women (30 out of 97). There were 12 Orthodox and 10 Roman Catholics, representing various youth organizations and ecumenical bodies. The Youth Department had selected 84 delegates, the WSCF 26, the YMCA 5, the YWCA 5, and the International Christian Youth Exchange 7. There was a total of 78 lay members from various churches. Considerable subsidy for youth travel and entertainment had been provided in the assembly budget. The chief speakers at the preparatory conference were Eugene C. Blake, W.A. Visser 't Hooft, Philip A. Potter, Albert H. van den Heuvel, Lukas Vischer and Paul Abrecht.

In addition to the official youth participants, the young generation was present in strength: 345 stewards — mostly from Sweden — provided domestic and technical services to the delegates and the staff and at the same time entered fully into youth discussions of the burning issues until late in the night; other students were brought under the title "Club '68" by the Swedish Student Christian Movement. Swedish students, who had marched from Stockholm to Uppsala, made it clear from the beginning, however, that they supported the World Council of Churches.

The general distrust of institution and bureaucracy made it hard going from the very first day of the pre-assembly meeting. Participants insisted on voting about their own programme. Several were not sure that they wanted to listen to distinguished leaders. A small minority, mainly continental European, had come with the intention of disrupting the proceedings. The whole youth delegation was clearly dissatisfied with its place in the Assembly itself. They resented the fact that they had no vote in the plenary sessions, although they appreciated the decision of the Central Committee that their corrective and creative presence was needed.

In the whole history of the ecumenical movement youth had never been so visibly present and clearly critical of adult deliberations as at the Uppsala Assembly. On the very first day, two of the youth participants were taken to the police headquarters where they were detained for three hours. They had sought to engage the spectators outside the cathedral in a discussion of the incongruity of such antiquated inaugural acts as a procession at an assembly meeting under the biblical theme: "Behold, I make all things new."

At the closing worship young people insisted upon their participation at very short notice. At the singing of the anthem "When I needed a neighbour", a group of demonstrators appeared, carrying placards. Printed on the placards were extracts from official enactments of the Assembly, voted by the delegates themselves. The message to the churches and their representatives was clear: Put up or shut up. Practise what you preach. Be ready for costly self-dedication. The visible participation was eloquently underlined by a youth leader who was invited to give the only short address at the closing service.

One method of youth involvement that had considerable impact was provided through "Hot News", a publication highly critical of all that went on, appearing every other day. ""Little Brother" asked embarrassing questions such as: "Can the churches be the breeeding ground for political solutions?... Do they hover above human life, or are they concerned with its essentials?... Can the churches find better means of communication and methods of action than those they use now? Will this conference be able to invent some and test them?"[1]

Stephen C. Rose wrote: "Perhaps this will be the last world assembly. In case there is another, let us pass an immediate resolution binding the WCC in the future to the elimination of youth participants in favour of delegations which contain at least 25 percent of persons under 35. Earlier Little Brother had noted that when W.A. Visser 't Hooft became the first General Secretary of the WCC he was 38; in those days the policymakers were much younger. Speaking in the name of hard-pressing youth, Théodore Buss expressed the conviction that the Uppsala Assembly stands or falls on the implementation of its results, and each one of us is sent back to his local church, to spread these results and to make all things new."[2]

Among the various proposals made by the youth in a statement distributed to the delegates was the recommendation that the churches should "discover the common service among the poor, the suffering and the exploited of the world as a way to the unity which demonstrates that we maintain the same apostolic faith, proclaim the same gospel, break the same bread, and unite in common prayer". Youth had not come as simple spectators, it asserted, nor to sanction a passive presence of the official churches, but to evolve a strategy of effective action to fight for peace and justice in the broken and hostile world. A number of other statements were circulated during the Assembly. Dealing with Section I "The Holy Spirit and the Catholicity of the Church", the youth delegation emphasized that "the Holy Spirit is the mutual acceptance of the responsibility to proclaim the message... The World Council of Churches is no more than the United Nations if it denies united worship and the celebration of the Eucharist of *all* assembly participants... without this communion there is no testimony."

Evaluating the many youth activities at Uppsala, Eugene C. Blake, the general secretary of the World Council of Churches 1966-72, came to the following conclusion: "The final resolutions of the youth participants were heard by the Assembly in plenary session on the last day. They were received with thanks but were not discussed. Generally speaking the concrete proposals of the youth participants on the subject before the

Assembly were neither better nor more 'radical' than the proposals officially before the Assembly backed by the authority of the central and other 'establishment' departmental and divisional committees."[3]

In an unpublished report "The Youth Participants at Uppsala", dated November 1968, Robert E. Maurer, chairman of the steering committee of the youth participants at the Assembly, made a stronger judgment on youth involvement in ecumenical matters. "The youth participants lacked, on the whole, the kind of background in which identification with the 'proletarian peoples of the world' would be more than a matter of words. To have sustained a struggle in Uppsala against the tendencies in the member churches and other institutions to maintain the status quo, the youth participants would have to come from similar struggles in their own countries. The lack of the 'wounds and pain' of political and theological struggle marked the inability of the youth participants to live up to their own mandate." The chairman admitted, however, that youth made one central and significant contribution: a new style of communication. The medium of youth expression was effective in a way its message never could have been. Yet, here also he did not hesitate to be critical. The three public forums of Club '68, Café Chantant and *Hot News* were not mainly the work of young delegates; the Swedish host students were primarily responsible for these "anti-establishment" manifestations. And they organized their own mini-bureaucracy for expediting their business. In a memorandum to Oscar Bolioli, dated 17 December 1968, Albert H. van den Heuvel stated "that the Maurer statement about the youth participants in Uppsala is pretty balanced", and encouraged his colleague to "make sure that a copy exists in the Assembly archives of the WCC".

It was not surprising that in the light of all this the report *Uppsala to Nairobi* also struck some disenchanting notes with regard to youth in the coming years. "At the time of the Upppsala Assembly the just course in attempting to respond to the vocal young people everywhere apparent seemed to be somehow to integrate youth and their concerns more organically into the whole working of the World Council of Churches. To say so was easy, and may have sounded easy to many, but the doing of it has proved difficult during the period under review. Even in 1968 the Youth Department noted that 'a real integration, which would require or at least allow critical participation, is more than most adults can take and more than most young people can muster'. Added to this problem were two other factors: first, some of the traditional structures by which Christian youth were related to the programmes of the WCC were beginning to experience some difficulties, such as rapid change in leadership and membership, as well as financial instability; and second, the Constitution and Rules of the WCC had not been devised to allow the participation of young people at the highest levels of leadership in any great number..."

From 1969 to 1973 the staff of the Youth Department was indeed greatly diminished and, due to financial reallocations, the Department lost access to those programme resources which were used to support the people who now took up other assignments. Funds for conducting ecumenical youth work administration by the headquarters in Geneva — outside of the Ecumenical Youth Service and world youth projects, both entirely financed by the Commission on Inter-Church Aid, Refugee and World Service with designated grants — were severely limited. Under the integration policy youth concerns and programmes were to be dealt with throughout the WCC, particularly within the Division of Ecumenical Action, from 1971 onwards within the Programme Unit on Education and Renewal. (This Unit was first called Education and Communication.) "Yet, in effect", according to the *Uppsala to Nairobi* report, "youth as a constituency was obscured and seemed to become the object of benign neglect".[4]

On the direct representation of young people in the governing organs of the World Council of Churches, the Central Committee at Canterbury in August 1969 resolved "to appoint to the next meeting of the Central Committee within the category of advisers not less than 15 and not more than 20 men and women under the age of 30. Nominations shall be made to the Executive Committee by member churches following a general invitation to the churches to submit nominations."[5] The practice was continued at subsequent meetings, and the younger advisers made substantial contributions to debates and decisions. At the Central Committee meeting in Addis Ababa, January 1971, specific provision was made for including youth in the supervisory committee for the Programme Unit on Education and Renewal, on the recommendation of the structure committee appointed by the Central Committee meeting at Rochester in 1963. It was decided that larger delegations to the Fifth Assembly must include young people. Nevertheless, the Central Committee had no authority to augment its own membership in favour of youth, and it was slow to ensure that a fair number of young men and women were made members of the Council's other commissions, committees and working groups.

It became apparent in the early seventies that the hoped-for involvement of youth in all aspects of the WCC's work was not being achieved, and there was no adequate response to the challenge so sharply posed by the young participants at the Uppsala Assembly and by their contemporaries in many parts of the world. The Central Committee meeting at

Utrecht in August 1972 noted the desire of what was then called the Renewal Group "to be authorized to pick up new concerns and experiment in new areas with a view to achieving" the discovery of "where and how God is acting today through traditional or new and radical movements in church and society, to facilitate communication between such movements, and to stimulate the churches to share in this quest". The Policy Reference Committee of the Central Committee particularly insisted "that there be a continuing commitment to youth within the World Council of Churches and that the proposal for a youth team be regarded as a way forward in WCC youth work".[6]

An *ad hoc* committee on youth was set up, and the following year the Central Committee expressed the hope "that every effort will be made to maintain and develop contacts with the regional activities in this field, so as to secure adequate participation of young people in the Fifth Assembly and more adequate plans for the post-Assembly period".[7] At its meeting in 1974, the Central Committee was not able to agree on the establishment of a special youth fund, but it did resolve "that the General Secretary be asked to examine the situation of youth work in the WCC afresh and bring proposals to the Executive Committee in April 1975".[8] An expanded staff group was assigned to carry out this mandate, and a special workshop of youth concerns was scheduled for the Nairobi Assembly.

What transpired during the year 1968 and after had wide-ranging implications for the ecumenical movement, the World Council and its member churches. The world situation was analyzed in *Uppsala to Nairobi* as follows: "Massive protests, students and young workers challenging the values (or lack of them) of an industrial order, just demands for a more human society and anti-war movements, all characterized an unprecedented epoch in the twentieth century that has given way to what the churches and society are now witnessing among the young, namely a quadrangle of moods: neo-conservatism; a silent, uninvolved majority; a confused, searching element; and a minority of activists. The nature and content of these 'moods' and movements differ markedly from region to region."[9]

The WCC Youth Department organized and sponsored considerably fewer consultations and conferences than in previous periods because ecumenical youth work became an increasingly hazardous enterprise. A series of encounters took place between younger Orthodox and Protestant theologians from 1965 onwards. The early intention was to bring Orthodox, particularly Greek Orthodox, young theologians out of their isolation. In 1970 there was Roman Catholic participation as well. That year an encounter in Italy studied "Man's Domestic Image". The technique developed at this consultation — literary texts were chosen as the focus of discussions — provided a common model for the sixth theological encounter between younger theologians of Orthodox, Protestant and Roman Catholic traditions at Cava dei Tirreni, Italy, 11-19 July 1970. At this meeting a play of informal discussion was staged and portions of "The Family Reunion" (T.S. Eliot), "Who's Afraid of Virginia Woolf" (Edward Albee), "The King of Asine and Helen" (George Seferis), "The Marriage of Karahmetis" (Papadiamantis) and "La cantatrice chauve" (E. Ionesco) were read and commented upon.[10]

Papers were read by James H. Cone, H. Assmann, P. Freire and E.I. Bodipo-Malumba at an international consultation on "Black Theology and Latin American Liberation Theology", held at Geneva, 1-4 May 1973. Participants were mainly Europeans from Western and some socialist countries. The symposium had extensive news coverage, and there was the full participation of over a dozen religious journalists. The heated debate never became a dialogue because of the nature of the issues presented. The contextual importance and historical conditioning of black theology and Latin American liberation theology were so different from European thought forms and experiences that it became quickly apparent how far the "oppressed" and the "oppressors" are isolated from each other in their experience and understanding of human life. The lack of dialogue — the title of the *Risk* number devoted to this symposium was "Incommunication" — presented a constant source of stimulation, frustration and challenge. Cone went so far as to state that "as long as we live in a world of oppressors and oppressed, communication is not possible". Several European participants took the rejection personally and their bewilderment was reflected in interviews and in their contributions to religious journals.[11]

A workshop on spirituality was held at Windsor Castle, England, 8-17 May 1975. This workshop traced the discussion on worship from the Uppsala Assembly to a consultation on "Worship in a Secular Age" in Geneva in 1969, and the Louvain Faith and Order conference in August 1971 which had a section on "Worship Today". In Section V on "Worship" at Uppsala it was stated: "...the Church is called to participate fully in Jesus Christ's reconciling work among men. In worship we enter God's battle against the demonic forces of this world which alienate man from his Creator and his fellow men, which imprison him in narrow nationalism or arrogant sectarianism, which attack his life through racism or class division, war and oppression, famine or disease, poverty or wealth, and which drive him to cynicism, guilt and despair. When we worship, God shows us that in this battle the final victory belongs to Jesus Christ."[12]

Involved in experimental worship at St George's Chapel, Windsor Castle, the question was what opportunities existed for youth to bring the real struggles and problems of daily life into worship. Rex Davies commented on the meeting: "For many, Windsor was a painful experience. It highlighted how different expectations can be, especially those of people who dream of a more brilliant worship which might free people for greater things, and those of people whose tradition gives a sense of stability, continuity and hope. The ambiguity of the chapel became a matter of pain: the eloquence of its architecture, which spoke to some of God's glory, told others of a history of torture and colonial oppression. There were too many tablets commemorating those who had fallen in the 'Indian Mutiny' for Jyoti Sahi to feel at ease. And the maleness of many of our accepted norms in worship precipitated a deep crisis for all. It was no longer possible to slide blindly past the pain women feel at the unthinking exclusion so carelessly imposed on them by men."[13]

The story of youth in Taizé, France, is a striking illustration of the deep search for meaning among young people in the late sixties and seventies in the midst of increased complexity and confusion. Brother Roger Schutz first came to the village of Taizé in 1940. He dreamt of starting a community, and he chose to do so in an area at that time strongly marked by human distress. During the war his house became a place of welcome for refugees, especially Jews, fleeing from Nazi occupation. At Easter 1949 seven brothers committed themselves to a life of celibacy and community. In 1953 Brother Roger completed "The Rule of Taizé". Many Protestants were suspicious of what appeared like Roman Catholic rules and practices. The Catholics themselves were slow to participate. After Roger Schutz was received in audience by Pope John XXIII in 1958, however, the community was asked to send its own observers to the Second Vatican Council. Since then members of Roman Catholic orders have shared in the life and work of Taizé.

In 1962 Christian young people from Germany built the large Church of Reconciliation in order to welcome the ever larger crowds visiting Taizé. Catholic and Orthodox chapels were built in the crypt. A large conference centre was added. In the twenty-fifth year after Schutz's arrival in the village, 200,000 people came to see what was now recognized as a prophetic sign at Taizé.

In September 1966 the first international youth meeting was held at Taizé. The second international gathering was attended by more than 1,600 young people from European countries, the United States and the third world, half Catholic and half Protestant. Eugene C. Blake, the general secretary of the World Council, spoke to the crowd: "We must be faithful to the deposit of the faith and to the transcendence of God, but at the same time radical in going beyond our styles, our manner of being and thinking." Divided into 60 groups, the participants had to consider the theme: "To Live". Four times they were asked a "surprise question" in order to stimulate first a personal and silent search, and then a dialogue. A declaration of the young people contained the words "...Reconciled in one universal community, Christians will be able to be a living word at the heart of the tragedies of war, injustice, segregation, and hunger."[14]

The preparation of the Council of Youth from 20 August to 1 September 1974, took four and a half years — an "inner adventure" before the "public adventure." Each year during the international meetings in Taizé a single theme was explored, to help each one, on returning home, to enter into this "inner adventure".

Forty thousand young people from one hundred countries gathered for the Council of Youth. A first letter of the people of God called upon the church to become a "universal community of sharing", a "people of the beatitudes". At the same time Brother Roger wrote a letter to each person, entitled "Living Beyond Every Hope". Successive letters were sent out in December of the following years from Calcutta, the China Sea, a slum in Mathare Valley, Kenya, and Latin America. At the Council of Youth, Pope Paul VI was represented by Cardinal Willebrands; the Patriarch of Constantinople by Metropolitan Emilianos; the Archbishop of Canterbury by Bishop Woods; and the World Council of Churches by Philip Potter.

In the acts of the Council of Youth it was recorded: "Either the people of God will remain fragmented into a multitude of splinter-groups, mutually opposed or indifferent, incapable of sharing the joys and sufferings of the entire human family. Then it will not be surprising that the men and women of our time turn from the church in ever greater numbers, and that she is replaced by indifference or by the ideologies of an imposed sharing. Or else Christians, rooted in the celebration of Christ dead and risen, will enter upon a process of reconciliation, rediscover a visible communion around a universal pastor, and widen their solidarity to include every human being."[15]

There were different evaluations of the Council of Youth and its impact during the following years. Jean Claude Grenier, a young French journalist, spoke openly of the ambiguity of the Taizé adventure.[16] The political ambiguity, he said, was matched by an ecumenical ambiguity. The celebration of the eucharist was insufficiently prepared and announced. There were two different tables, one for Roman Catholics and one for

Protestants. In the last moment, however, the hosts on the two tables were mixed. The growing indifference of youth towards ecumenism was reinforced in spite of the best intentions of the Taizé brothers.

Specific youth ministries were carried out by the World Council through the Ecumenical Youth Service and the world youth projects. In Europe much attention was paid to social service and community organization, in particular in larger satellite cities in England and Germany.

World youth projects varied greatly in scope and purpose. Besides providing for leadership training in various continents and regions and the education of secretaries for youth departments of national Christian councils, financial support was given to cooperative youth programmes, particularly in Asia.

The Ecumenical Youth Council in Europe was formed in 1968 as the expression of a concern for regionalization in the ecumenical movement. The EYCE was from the beginning eager to find ways of cooperation with the World Council of Churches, the Conference of European Churches and secular youth organizations in Europe. Close relations were established with the European section of the WSCF. All national ecumenical youth bodies have become members of the EYCE, and even in those churches where there is no organized youth movement, there is still some relationship with the EYCE. Working contacts have been intensified with the Christian Peace Conference, the International Christian Youth Exchange, SYNDESMOS, the Methodist Youth Council in Europe, the Young Men's Christian Association, and other organizations.

The Council does not see itself as representing the young generation in Europe, but rather as a forum or platform for dialogue and encounter. It openly admits that there are considerable tensions, contradictions and antagonisms in its ranks in theological and political matters. But there is a feeling among young people and among youth leaders that though the situation is not bright in the East and the West, there are certain things which hold the youth together as Christians.

The Preamble of the Constitution of the EYCE reads as follows:

> The Ecumenical Youth Council in Europe is a fellowship of national ecumenical youth councils, denominational youth councils or bodies and those representing church youth in Europe which accept Jesus Christ as Lord and Saviour according to the scriptures and therefore seek to serve him and thereby to serve mankind.
>
> The Council works in a continent where there are many social and political systems and a variety of denominational traditions. It recognizes that there are tensions and problems in this situation and commits itself to the

task of overcoming them and of establishing a deeper understanding and fellowship between young people in the name of Jesus Christ.

After taking over the responsibilities for ecumenical youth service (ecumenical work camps) in 1972 from the Youth Sub-unit of the World Council of Churches, the EYCE has recently made some far-reaching organizational changes in this programme. The national youth councils have assumed full responsibility for the camps taking place in their countries. There has been a clear extension of the programme with the incorporation of Eastern and Southern Europe.

In 1975, the EYCE organized a European ecumenical youth conference in Driebergen, Holland. There were 150 participants. The theme was "Faith Today". In 1978 a second conference of this kind was held in France around the theme "Change and be Changed", and in 1982 a third took place in the GDR under the theme "Faith and Justice".

NOTES

[1] No. 1, 3 July 1968, p.3.
[2] *Hot News*, No. 8, 19 July 1968, p.8.
[3] "Uppsala and Afterwards", in *The Ecumenical Advance: a History of the Ecumenical Movement*, Vol. 2, 1948-1968, ed. Harold E. Fey, London, SPCK, 1970, pp.416-417.
[4] *Uppsala to Nairobi, 1968-1975*, ed. David E. Johnson, New York, Friendship Press and London, SPCK, 1975, p.200.
[5] *Minutes and Reports*, Geneva, WCC, 1969, p.33.
[6] *Minutes and Reports*, Geneva, WCC, 1972, pp.36-37.
[7] *Minutes and Reports*, Geneva, WCC, 1973, p.48.
[8] *Minutes*, Geneva, WCC, 1974, p.47.
[9] *Op.cit.*, p.202.
[10] *Encounter at Cava*, Geneva, WCC Division of Ecumenical Action, Youth Department, 1970.
[11] *Risk*, Vol. 9, No. 2, 1973.
[12] *The Uppsala Report 1968*, ed. Norman Goodall, Geneva, WCC, 1968, p.79.
[13] *Risk*, Vol. 12, No. 2, 1976, p.25.
[14] *Ecumenical Youth News*, No. 7, September 1967, p.2.
[15] *Letter from Taizé*, No. 59-60, July-August 1979, p.33.
[16] *Taizé — une aventure ambiguë*, Paris, Ed. du Cerf, 1975.

VIII. Nairobi 1975-

Before the Fifth Assembly of the World Council of Churches met in Nairobi, young people, representing their churches and Christian youth organizations, met in Arusha, Tanzania, from 16 to 22 November, for a pre-Assembly youth conference. The gathering was of great value to the group. It produced a statement which focused on the inability of governments to resolve the acute economic problems of the day. The so-called developed nations need the national resources and the labour of the poor in the underdeveloped countries to maintain themselves. These poor are "ruthlessly exploited with the complicity of totalitarian regimes in which torture, imprisonment, and even physical elimination are common methods of governments".

It is important to note that an agreement was reached at the beginning of the Nairobi Assembly that the moderators of the two workshops (on spirituality and on youth) should become members of the Assembly Business Committee. The workshop on youth was asked to select a person under 30 to be its member on the Assembly Business Committee. The Programme Guidelines Committee received the reports from the workshops on spirituality and youth.

The report on the youth workshop, which was discussed in an Assembly Hearing on Unit III, Education and Renewal, contained several new elements. The aim of youth work was spelled out as follows: "Youth work in the World Council of Churches should be organized so as to enable youth together to discover for themselves the freedom and unity of Christ, to voice their concerns and insights effectively, and to participate at all levels of the ecumenical movement, particularly in the WCC. The focus should seek to bring the challenges and concerns of youth into the central life of the WCC in all aspects of its work."

To this end a change in the structure of the Council was suggested: "Youth work must have a somewhat autonomous character, structurally located in one particular Programme Unit, but relating to all units so as to bring the presence and concerns of youth fully into the life of the ecumenical movement. Therefore, it is proposed that a sub-unit on youth with a committee for youth work be created, related to Programme Unit II where there exists a natural link, having priorities for Education and Renewal."

The report of the youth workshop helped the participants in Hearing 4 on Unit III to "emphasize the following concrete issues for further study and action: (1) youth participation in ecumenism on local and international levels; (2) youth for social justice: (a) youth and personhood, (b) violence and non-violence, (c) youth and spirituality".[1] In the following years youth and theology, youth and education, youth and social justice were identified as three major areas of concern.

High priority was also given to making contacts with youth and youth leaders around the world and to building a network of communication among them. Encounters with young people took place through various channels: youth workers and others in the member churches and national councils of churches; regional contacts; other international Christian youth movements including the YMCA, YWCA, WSCF, Intervarsity Fellowship, Roman Catholic and Orthodox organizations, in particular SYNDESMOS, the World Fellowship of Orthodox Youth Organizations, and other interested individuals and groups. The Sub-unit on Youth became involved in much correspondence and travel to meet as many people as possible. From 1977 onwards a newsletter, sharing information about the World Council and other youth programmes, was distributed within the constituency.

In its relation to regional partners, questions of regional autonomy and the question of programme priorities had to be faced. It marked the beginning of a new stage of collaboration, based on a clearer understanding of the privileges and responsibilities which partnership implies.

The Christian Conference of Asia (CCA) has in its region the largest section of the world's population and therefore of the world's young. From 1975 onwards special programmes were evolved for rural youth in the region. In the large rural areas there were obvious problems of unemployment, rapid population growth, wasted resources and widespread poverty. The Youth Department of the CCA initiated programmes or supported already existing projects that released the productive energies of rural youth, met specific needs in rural communities and carried forward the basic task of conscientization for political action. The training of a cadre of committed and disciplined rural youth workers and organizers was now a specific goal.

It was recognized that young people had to be exposed to varying models of rural development. Countries like Taiwan, Malaysia and the Philippines try to promote rural development through massive technical inputs and foreign investments spilling over into agro-industries or agro-capitalism. Countries like Sri Lanka, India and Pakistan have limited land reform and have initiated experiments in collective farming within the context of mixed economy.

The swift dismantling of colonialism in several parts of Africa, the gathering storm in countries where racist oppression continued, the support to liberation movements by the World Council of Churches — all these became a preoccupation of the youth department of the All Africa Conference of Churches (AACC). As African young people were aware that national governments themselves behave like the oppressive regimes of colonial times and are guilty of the violation of human rights, the concept and models of leadership training had to be re-examined. Not only was there an agonizing search for an African identity in the churches; efforts had to be made to raise the consciousness of young people so as to get them fully involved in the development process and in the struggle against many forms of racism and colonialism. As African countries had far more contacts with the former colonial powers than among themselves, importance was given to regional visitation and to trainers' exchange programmes.

The name Latin American Union of Evangelical Youth (ULAJE) was changed in 1970 to the Latin American Union of Ecumenical Youth. Increasingly young people from the Roman Catholic Church participated in this regional body. It redefined its aim as being a bridge between the young generation and the old, between church people and non-church people, both engaged in the common task of resisting oppression and exploitation and changing the structures of a totalitarian society. Youth work became understood as committed ecumenism and involvement in the process of the liberation of people. The two major areas of work are still with marginalized urban youth and with rural youth in predominantly rural countries. Priority is given to community organizations. Other projects undertaken by ULAJE are documentation centres, popular theatres, youth training and leadership courses.

The Caribbean Conference of Churches has the distinction of having the Roman Catholic Church in its membership. This gives its youth department special challenges and opportunities. It realizes that it cannot address itself only to issues of individual youth groups in the churches, or to matters of differences in doctrine and counselling. With an emphasis on self-reliance and self-development, it has given priority to pro-

grammes which will equip the youth to struggle against cultural deprivation, institutionalized racism and dependence on the tourist dollar.

Fifty percent of the population in the Middle East are below 25 years of
age. The newly created youth department of the Middle East Council of
Churches defined the most urgent concern of Christian youth in that
region as being twofold: (1) the support of Israel by Western powers —
partly based on their sense of guilt — and the denial of basic human rights
and justice to the uprooted Palestinian people; and (2) the question of
identity vis-à-vis their own churches, the Christian communities and the
Arab nations as a whole. The inability of churches to respond positively
to the demands of social change, religious liberty and dialogue with
people of other faiths had to be continuously challenged.

The three groups of islands, Melanesia, Micronesia and Polynesia
comprising the Pacific region vary greatly in geographical characteristics,
history, language and customs. Yet special interests bind these thousands
of islands together. Among them are the concern for a nuclear-free Pacific
and the recognition of the dangers of tourism. The Pacific Conference of
Churches had become keenly aware of the role of young men and women
in the planning of their future. In order to meet the changes that need to be
faced and at the same time to maintain tradition in homes, villages, cities,
schools, business and governmental institutions, one must recognize the
challenge of Christ to the old and the young alike. The Pacific churches
youth convention on the theme "Challenged by Christ" in Suva, Fiji, in
January 1980 was the first event of its kind.

Three significant gatherings organized by the WCC's Sub-unit on
Youth took place in 1977 and 1978. An international conference was held
in Bossey, 25 August-4 September 1977, on the theme "Christian
Witness for Social Justice". A regional ecumenical seminar on "Christian
Youth in a Troubled Society" in the monastery of Ayia Napa in Cyprus,
13-20 July 1978, was organized jointly with the Middle East Council of
Churches. During the summer of 1978 a student course was held in
Bossey on the theme "Christian Vigilance and Solidarity on Six Conti-
nents". The course was co-sponsored by the World Student Christian
Federation, the Programme on Theological Education and the Ecumenical
Institute.

The word festivals for youth and students, which started after the
Second World War, were an attempt by youth to unite their efforts in the
struggle for peace. At first, the festivals depended upon the support of the
World Federation of Democratic Youth and the International Students'
Union and were held in socialist countries. Since the 1950s, the festivals
gained in importance, and in 1959 one was held in Austria, and another in

Finland. A large number of international organizations with different political, social and religious orientations now began to participate in the festivals.

The eleventh world festival for youth and students was held in Cuba, 28 July-5 August 1978. A wide variety of countries and organizations was represented by some 18,500 delegates from all over the world. A fair number of the organizations were Christian: YWCA, YMCA, WSCF, WCC, Christian Peace Conference (CPC), ULAJE. Well-known Christian leaders like Bishop Sergio Mendez Arcea of Cuernavaca, Mexico, addressed the gathering.

In the discussions of the Council's Youth Office on regional programmes and priorities, it became clear that the major emphasis in each region was on questions of faith and justice today: what it means to be a Christian today, and how to struggle together for justice, both in local situations and globally. This emphasis was reflected in all the programmes — regional, inter-regional and international — which were being planned. In the light of this development the Central Committee decided in 1980 not to hold a world youth conference in 1981, although it had fully supported in 1979 the youth working group's proposal for such a major international gathering and to endorse the planning of multiple events under the general theme of faith and justice.[2]

Several regional youth gatherings took place from 1979 to 1981. ULAJE organized a Latin American regional meeting in July 1979 on the theme "Theology and Youth Ministries". A regional meeting in Botswana, March 1980, discussed the theme "The Role of Youth and Nation Building"; a regional meeting in Syria, March 1981, focused on "To be a Servant". "Renewal and the Liberation of the Oppressed" was the theme of a conference held in Cyprus, 1-8 August 1980, organized by the All Africa Conference of Churches, the Ecumenical Youth Council in Europe and the Middle East Council of Churches youth constituencies, in cooperation with the World Council's Youth Sub-unit. Fifty participants representing eight regions and SYNDESMOS attended a final international course on "Faith and Justice", in Turin, Italy, 17-25 June 1981.

The constituency of the youth office was involved in three major conferences of the World Council of Churches. Ten young people participated as consultants in the commission meeting of Faith and Order in Bangalore, India, 15-30 August 1978, and contributed to the discussion of the themes "Giving Account of the Hope that is in Us", and "Growing Together into Unity".

The youth report stated: "Youth should not be regarded as a special category — they are fully a part of the people of God; nor are they the 'church of tomorrow', but members of today's church. They are not confined to so-called youth issues, but as part of the universal community of faith confront all the problems facing humanity today." Concerning the life of the church the following conviction was expressed: "There is a tension in our thinking about the church — a tension between what the church actually is and what the church is called to become. The focus of our involvement in the life of the church is precisely at such points of tension. We affirm that in order to be credible the church must be endowed with a great spiritual independence. The church can be credible only if its international and external life is prepared to carry the cross of Jesus rather than merely preaching it; if in the big battles of life it is prepared to renounce success and dwell on service; if it will embody Christian hope by showing freedom or judgment and courage to go against the tide."[3]

Prior to the world conference on "Faith, Science and the Future", held in Cambridge, Massachusetts, 12-24 July 1979, seventy students of natural and social sciences, and other young people involved in community organization, trade unions, journalism, etc., met at Wellesley, Massachusetts. They issued an extensive report. Among other things, it said: "What is needed is a new vision of a global community, a new society in which the horizons of moral concern and accountability extend not only to every human, but also to every other aspect of the natural order... The greatest part of scientific research and the development and use of technology should be directed towards meeting basic human needs..."[4]

"Your Kingdom Come" was the theme of the world conference on mission and evangelism, held in Melbourne, Australia, 12-25 May 1980. Youth delegates and stewards met in a pre-consultation on 10 May. There was also a "Youth for Mission and Evangelism" conference at the House of the Gentle Bunyip. The youth associated themselves in particular with the recommendations from the conference Section I to the World Council's member churches that they (1) become churches in solidarity with the poor; (2) join the struggle against the forces of impoverishment; (3) establish new relationships with the poor inside the churches; (4) pray and work for the kingdom of God.

The assembly of the Christian Conference of Asia at Bangalore in May 1981, the assembly of the All Africa Conference of Churches in July 1981, and the assembly of the Caribbean Conference of Churches in Curacao, November 1981, were all preceded by youth assemblies, helping young delegates to familiarize themselves with issues and prepare themselves for full participation.

During 1981-82 the Sub-unit on Youth worked actively to ensure a reasonable presence of young people at the Sixth WCC Assembly which was held in Vancouver from 24 July to 10 August 1983. Unfortunately the Sub-unit had only limited success in obtaining a sufficient number of names of qualified young people from the regions. In spite of this, over 13 percent of the delegates at Vancouver were under 30, in comparison with 9 percent at Nairobi, and 4 percent (under 35) at Uppsala. The youth office insisted on the inclusion of young people in the large number of ecumenical team visits that preceded the Assembly. It also organized a series of youth-to-youth visits which ran parallel to the team visits and made possible meaningful contacts with large numbers of young people who otherwise would not have the opportunity to participate in the process of preparation.

A pre-Assembly youth event took place, 17-21 July 1983, at the Vancouver School of Theology on the campus of the University of British Columbia where later the Assembly itself was held. The event brought together a total of 350 young people — youth delegates from the Council's member churches, stewards for the Assembly, youth advisers, representatives of youth organizations and Council staff. The 150 stewards carried more responsibility than ever before, helping with press, registration, reception and the travel desk, documentation, meeting rooms, plenaries, telephone and switchboard, general administration, mail sorting, message running and personal assistance to conference officers. For the first time there were "language stewards", helping informally with interpretation.

Addressing the pre-Assembly youth gathering Philip Potter reminded the participants of the various contributions made by the youth to the ecumenical movement. After the war young people were involved in acts of reconciliation through ecumenical work camps in Europe and Asia. They "were deeply involved in issues of the renewal of the church — the church being the 'laos', the laity, the whole people of God". They were the first to share the idea of ecumenical sharing of resources by starting world youth projects. "It was through the Youth Department that the Orthodox were invited to meet together to form SYNDESMOS... it was the youth who brought Roman Catholics as youth consultants to assemblies." Youth has been in the forefront of the issues of justice. A further contribution has been to promote regional ecumenism. "Even before the formation of regional councils of churches, there existed ecumenical youth organizations. Latin America and Europe are examples of this."[5]

The message from the pre-Assembly youth event to the Sixth Assembly contained the words:

We want peace:

NOT as the doctrine of national security defines it: repression, covert violence, the absence of war,

BUT as God's shalom built on justice;

NOT as the escalation of nuclear armaments,

BUT as the affirmation of human dignity and the meeting of basic human needs;

NOT as comfort and complacency,

BUT as gospel-rooted conviction and action.

We recognize that we ourselves are caught up in the structures of oppression and alienation, and at the same time we express our gratitude to God for those of us who are participating in the liberating struggles. We come with anguish and the desire to be instruments of the manifest power of the gospel.[6]

Regional statements from Asia, the Caribbean, Europe, the Middle East, Latin America, North America and the Pacific, with specific recommendations, were presented at the pre-Assembly event. Also a statement from the youth participants in the Assembly was issued stressing in particular that the right of sovereignty of all indigenous people in Canada be included in the new constitution of the nation and calling on the Canadian Council of Churches to speak and act in support of the demands.

At the end of the first session of cluster reports, Brother Roger of the Taizé community reflected on the relevance of the theme "Jesus Christ — the Life of the World" for the younger generation. So many of the young, he said, have been scarred by broken relationships and have lost the confident trust that is essential for life. "They yearn to find places of struggle and contemplation that anticipate forgiveness, communion and reconciliation. The resources of the ecumenical movement should be focused on a pastoral concern to enable each person to reconcile in him- or herself the irreplaceable treasures of the Orthodox churches, with the specific gifts of the Protestant churches, with all the charisms of the Catholic Church."[7]

In the discussion of Issue I, "Witnessing in a Divided World", it was noted that "the Gospel message becomes a transforming power within the life of a community when it is expressed in the cultural forms in which the community understands itself". Youth can contribute to the search for a theological understanding of culture and to a new ecumenical agenda in which various cultural expressions of the Christian faith may be in conversation with one another. There is need to analyze the influence of various kinds of religious movements on the life of young people.

In the report on Issue III, "Moving Towards Participation", it was stated: "Young people who are an integral part of the people of God have special gifts to offer: enthusiasm, fresh ways of looking at life, the willingness to challenge structures. They are however, often perceived as lacking in experience and an understanding of how the church functions. Tradition too is interpreted in such a way as to give older generations an unfair advantage. This leads to mutual misunderstanding, frustration on the part of youth and sometimes their rejection of the church. Opportunities which exist for dialogue need to be encouraged."

In the same Issue report the following recommendations on young people were made:

> 1. National and regional ecumenism is at a low ebb in many places. Churches are asked to make a much greater effort to build up ecumenical groups in order to give visibility to church unity.
>
> 2. In 1985, the International Youth Year, churches are asked to arrange programmes that will focus on youth, the witness by youth and unity among young people, bearing in mind the theme for the year: "Participation, Development, Peace".
>
> 3. It is recommended that churches give better opportunity for young people to move towards the centre of the work of the WCC. This should include representing their churches at WCC programmes, meetings and committees.
>
> 4. The churches and ecumenical youth should organize their work more closely with campus ministries and university chaplaincies in order to strengthen ecumenism among students and their involvement in the WCC.[8]

* * *

Ecumenical work camps, as we have seen, were one of the earliest programmes organized by the World Council of Churches. Starting in Europe in the aftermath of the Second World War, they enabled young people to meet and work together for reconstruction and reconciliation. The early camps involved a good deal of manual work; social service projects then emerged as the youth tried to respond more fully to the needs of society. The camp tasks varied enormously — from construction work to helping with mentally handicapped people, from adventure playgrounds to ecology schemes. And the spirit of voluntary service and the experience of community living made a great impact both on the volunteers and the places where they worked.

During the seventies many changes took place. The whole European programme was moved from the World Council of Churches to the Ecumenical Youth Council in Europe in 1972. In recent years no camps have been conducted in Latin America or the Caribbean within the programme. A few camps continued to be held in Asia, but most were in Africa. The camps were mainly in the rural areas and designed to help in national developments, e.g. development of agricultural land, digging of wells, construction of clinics and health centres.

Several years ago Ecumenical Youth Service (EYS) had come under criticism; it was accused of promoting elitism and failing to fulfill the expectation of ecumenical encounters. The Central Committee of the Council called for a full evaluation of the programme. Administrative responsibilities were transfered to the regional bodies in 1980. New criteria for the programme need to be worked out and sources of funding identified for the revitalized programme.

World Youth Projects (WYP) are also still a part of the programme of the Sub-unit. They are designed for young people, involving the partici- pants in a mutual sharing of needs and resources to develop and streng- then ecumenical youth work around the world. Through exchange of funds, ideas and material it is a means of equipping denominational, national and regional youth secretaries, youth organizations and youth groups with resources to develop a strategy for youth work in their areas in a way that is relevant to their situation and enables young people to participate fully in the true development of their community and their country.

The projects are initiated and carried through by local, national and regional groups and organizations. While each region determines its own priorities — and therefore the selection of partners — there are some overall guidelines given by WYP as to the kind of work which could be included in this programme. The Sub-unit is responsible in helping to find funds — projects are listed through the channels of the Commission of Inter-Church Aid, Refugee and World Service — and publishing a global report on projects and for circulating the reports to donors and to the regions. Departing from the traditional concept of screening projects in isolation, WYP seeks instead to support local, national, regional and global programmes through a continuing process of dialogue and mutual accountability. An evaluation of WYP is planned in all of the eight regions. National bodies in Africa and Asia have already completed the evaluation.

An ecumenical team of young people from seven countries including Hong Kong travelled in the summer of 1984 to four provinces in China, visiting churches and Christian young people in Nanjing, Shanghai, Fouzhou and Guamgzhou. It was the first time such a visit was under- taken. The team included representatives from the Christian Conference of Asia youth department, the WCC's Sub-unit on Youth, the World Student Christian Federation's Asia-Pacific region, the Asia alliance of the YMCAs, the Hong Kong Christian Council youth department and the Tao Fong Shan ecumenical centre. The team was planned as an Asian ecumenical youth leaders visitation to build ecumenical relations with Chinese Christian young people and to share Asian concerns. The visit was coordinated by the Christian Conference of Asia youth department with the China Christian Council and the Three Self Patriotic Movement.[9]

Asian Christian young people gathered in Delhi, 25 September-10 October 1984 around the theme "Thy Will Be Done". Sponsored by the youth department of the Christian Conference of Asia, the assembly brought together 270 youth from all over the continent. Its sessions set a significant agenda for the involvement of young Asian Christians in the social issues which face their societies. An important feature of this assembly was that half a dozen young people from Peru, Tuvalu, the Netherlands, Canada and the United States also participated in it.

Before going to Delhi, assembly participants made an ecumenical team visit through India, which took them to Calcutta, Raipur, Bombay, Goa, Hyderabad, Madras, Bangalore, Trivandrum and Madurai. The purpose of the visit was to expose the delegates to some of the issues facing young people, through meetings with a cross-section of the poor in Indian society — the untouchables and the urban poor, industrial workers and landless labourers, fishermen and quarry workers, tribal people and women, peasant organizations and Tamil refugees from Sri Lanka.

* * *

A note on national and international Christian youth movements and organizations. There are over 500 Christian organizations ministering to youth which are of major significance at national or wider levels. Among the Roman Catholic bodies are the Grail (International Movement of Catholic Laywomen), the Legion of Mary (Association of Lay Roman Catholics), the International Catholic Youth Federation (ICYF), and Pax Romana (International Movement of Roman Catholic Students). Young Christian Students (YCS) and Young Christian Workers (YCW) were created in Belgium in 1925. Mention should also be made of the Focolare movement which from 1944 onwards, under the guidance of Chiara Lubich, has spread to many parts of the world. Its aim is to promote Christian unity, particularly among the young. Youth for Christ International (YFCI) was organized in the United States in 1945. The *World*

Christian Encyclopedia lists 30 youth organizations in Great Britain and 28 youth organizations in the United States.[10]

There is indeed no lack of Christian bodies ministering throughout the world to the needs of youth. But the question may be raised as to whether their traditions and structures hinder them rather than help them in developing a new sensitivity to the ever-changing aspirations of the young generation. Their outlook and function can become as anachronistic and irrelevant as those of adult Christian institutions unless they face the challenges of the times.

NOTES

[1] *Breaking Barriers: Nairobi 1975*, ed. David M. Paton, London, SPCK, and Grand Rapids, Wm. B. Eerdmans, 1976, p.310.
[2] *Minutes*, Geneva, WCC, 1981, pp.84-85.
[3] *Youth Newsletter*, Vol. 2, No. 3, December 1978, pp.32-35.
[4] "Report on the Science Students Conference", *Faith and Science in an Unjust World*, Volume 2: Reports and Recommendations, ed. Paul Abrecht, Geneva, WCC, 1980, p.173.
[5] *Youth Newsletter*, Vol. 7, No. 3, September 1983, p.5.
[6] *Ibid.*, p.6.
[7] *Gathered for Life*, ed. David Gill, Geneva, WCC and Grand Rapids, Eerdmans, 1983, p.27.
[8] *Ibid.*, pp.33, 41, 56, 58-59.
[9] *Youth Newsletter*, Vol. 8, No. 3, September 1984.
[10] Ed. David B. Barrett, Nairobi, Oxford University Press, 1982, p.971.

IX. The Past, the Present and the Future

What we say in this final chapter about the present situation of the young generation does not apply only to the World Council and its constituency; all churches, including the Roman Catholic Church, are aware of the fact that too many young people are marginalized, isolated from older generations and alienated from social structures.

As this book shows, the involvement of youth in the ecumenical movement from 1925 onwards, and in the World Council of Churches from 1948 onwards, has gone through five successive stages — the early period of a partnership, of a more or less single and visible community of two generations; the emergence of a world Christian youth community; the call for the integration of youth in the life of the established church and the participation of youth in the mission and service of the church; the conflict between the older and younger generations; and the contemporary situation where the Christian youth wish to witness in their own ways to God's freedom and to be the church in their own sector of the world's life.

Although the sixties were the most exciting, creative and controversial period, all stages were marked by trial and error, advancement and stagnation, whether young people were in agreement or in conflict with — or indifferent to — the church.

Church and youth join forces

The late twenties and the thirties were marked by the common conviction that Christianity is a youth movement, that Christianity and youth are global partners, and that the church and youth must join forces. In spite of the wilderness experience of war and economic depression, the threat of totalitarian ideologies and the increasing impact of secularization, there was the deep conviction that Christianity will still be spreading and that its great days are ahead and not behind. From youth will come the leadership for the next advance of the Christian faith. It has its future before it.

Despite the tragedies that marked the period, Christian leaders were convinced that the worldwide church would continue as a vital reality across the boundaries of nation, race, denomination and political difference. The outreach of Christianity was now a global fact. There was no land to which the Christian message had not been carried. Although in Europe church membership had decreased, the churches had become more aware of their future vocation and task. In Latin America the churches, especially the Protestant churches, grew in number and influence. Christians in Asia, though a small minority, carried a certain weight. More than ten million Christian young people in the United States had joined hands in the United Christian Youth Movement in 1934 under the slogan: "Build Today for a Christian World".

Indeed the time had come for youth to express their highest international ideals in terms of concrete and fearless action for understanding and friendship. They would move forward more rapidly in international cooperation than their elders. The enthusiasm of young communists to build a better world had to be both emulated and challenged. Nazi youth, who had been taught that Christianity in the Fatherland was the relic of an evil past, a corruption of the German spirit through Jewish influence, could be won back to follow the risen Lord of history. Opponents of Christianity were not only to be "out-thought" but "out-proclaimed", not only "out-lived" but "out-loved".

Christian youth in Europe, to be sure, were facing several serious problems. A kind of sexual revolution had started already in the twenties. Church leaders were worried about unrestrained relationships between boys and girls, moral relativism, venereal diseases in schools. In education empirical sciences were hailed as the basis of all verifiable knowledge. The time had come to challenge various atheistic and agnostic attitudes. Industrial society was in dire need of social laws to keep in check the exploitation of the manual labour of children and young people. In spite of the bitter experiences of the First World War, narrow and aggressive nationalism was again on the rise. Conscientious objection to military service and resistance to any kind of war had become key ecumenical issues. Peace was beginning to be conceived, not as the absence of war, but as the consequence of justice and equality.

These and other concerns were taken up in successive stages by the ecumenical youth commission of the World Alliance for International Friendship through the churches and the Universal Christian Council for Life and Work. Pursuing "its momentous objective", in collaboration with the other international youth movements, "to build a spiritually united church, vigorously responsive to its social duty", it was deeply aware of the fact that "the ecumenical enterprise, because of its nature, cannot be artificially superimposed from an international centre", but must be developed "in response to genuine desire in the actual local and national situations where its application is required."

The world Christian youth community

The first world conference of Christian youth at Amsterdam in 1939 was a great success. The Ecumenical Youth Commission had gathered together almost fifteen hundred Christian youth to share together in "the growing concerns of the whole ecumenical movement", and "to hear and to follow the clear call of God".[1] Looking back to the international gathering soon after the war S. Franklin Mack wrote: "*Christus Victor* came to stand as a supreme symbol of oneness. *Youth* had brought this about, *Christian* youth: youth undismayed by the bigness of the undertaking, undeterred by the imminent threat of war in Europe, confident that every problem has a Christian solution."[2] There was also the proud record of the WSCF within which the oneness of the Christian fellowship was preserved unbroken across the lines of division throughout the war.

Oslo 1947 could not repeat Amsterdam 1939. But it was the first major post-war gathering of Christian youth from all parts of the world and it marked the beginning of another stage in the involvement of youth in the ecumenical movement. It was encouraging that a large second world conference of Christian youth could be organized so soon after the war in a country disrupted by Nazi occupation. Many of the delegates from Europe and Asia had suffered five years of terror and hardship. But a spirit of forgiveness, reconciliation and solidarity dominated the conference. There was a demand for new leadership in the youth movements of many nations and an eagerness to meet this demand.

It was no less surprising that a delegation of one hundred young people attended the First Assembly of the World Council of Churches at Amsterdam in 1948, participating in the plenary sessions and organizing an intensive programme on its own. A delegate from the British West Indies, Philip A. Potter, said: "We sincerely hope that every facility will be afforded the Youth Department to help young Christians throughout the world to a clearer and more moving understanding of the World Church... Pentecost brought power to those who had seen God's design. Power — its nature, its use, its manifestations in peace and war —has forced itself upon our thoughts during these days. And if we realized our own impotence we knew also in penitence that this was caused by our imperfect obedience to God. With you, therefore, we resolve to go forth from here with the vision of the compelling and consuming task before us, and yet with the assurance that our sufficiency is of God."[3]

This vision indeed inspired the Youth Department from 1948 onwards. Its staff became deeply involved in reconstruction in Europe, revitalizing church youth work in spiritual and material realms. The annual European youth leaders conferences were carefully prepared and their recommendations and decisions carried out as far as possible. The youth training courses at the Ecumenical Institute at Bossey were well attended.

Eastern Europe in its ideological isolation became a focus of direct contact and regular activity; the concerns for creative youth work in Latin America and Asia, and later in Africa and the Middle East, were explored. A truly international outlook characterized the work of the Youth Department. The need for closer relationships with the International Missionary Council was clearly recognized.

The timely decision to set up a joint youth department committee of the World Council of Churches and the World Council of Christian Education and Sunday School Association had far-reaching consequences, in particular for a close and regular cooperation between North America and Europe. Relations with the leaders of Orthodox youth were cultivated. The wide network of friendship and unity, which the Youth Department consciously promoted, led to the establishment of SYNDESMOS in 1953.

News Sheet, published by the Youth Department from 1947 onwards, contained much information on the expectations, the excitement and the driving force of the staff and the constituency of the Youth Department. The personal contributions of the first executive secretary, Jean Fraser, and of the second executive secretary, Bengt-Thure Molander, testify in particular to the freedom and enthusiasm of those early years.

The worldwide enterprise of youth corresponded remarkably with the outlook, the hope and the strategy of the mature leaders of the ecumenical movement. It is revealing to recall how the Central Committee, meeting at Rolle, Switzerland, in 1951, around the themes "The Calling of the Church to Mission and Unity" and "The Role of the WCC in Times of Tension" defined the term "ecumenical". "It is important to insist that this word... is properly used to describe everything that relates to the whole task of the whole church to bring the Gospel to the whole world." Preparing for the Second Assembly the Rolle gathering stated that "Christ delivers the church from worldliness and isolation", that "Christ overcomes our disunity", that "Christ is the hope of powerless and persecuted churches", and that Christ is the centre of "the Church's witness to the world situation".[4] All these had to be achieved through and with the participation of the young generation in its own ecumenical context.

The integration of youth in the life and mission of the church

A third period of development and change in the consciousness and concerns of youth begins with Evanston 1954. Active after the Second Assembly of the World Council within the Division of Ecumenical Action, the Youth Department now tried out a new style of work. Not only did it continue to deepen ecumenical fellowship among Christian young people and to strengthen the youth work of the churches around the world, but it followed up its mandate "to keep before the churches their responsibility for the evangelization of young people and their growth in the Christian faith". The overall study theme "The Integration of Youth in the Life and Mission of the Church" served as a guiding principle of orientation and action.

Increasingly, however, questions were debated among youth as to what kind of life and fellowship the church offers. In what way can they actively take part in the community activities of the local congregation? Should not parish ecumenism, if it is to include them, be far more concretely an expression of local community-building that makes the values of Christian life credible? Gradually a deep disillusionment set in over the aloofness and the complacency of the established churches. Youth lost in particular its patience over the slowness and indifference of church leaders in the matter of a common celebration of the eucharist. The objections against inter-communion were to them a clear sign that the Christian communities would not easily go beyond the boundaries of their denominational settings. Renewal, leading to the breaking down of the theological and psychologi-cal fences around the table of the Lord, was resisted because of the widespread unwillingness to review sacramental theology and ecclesiasti-cal discipline in the light of the new ecumenical vision.

Youth also felt that the sacrament of baptism as God's action in human history had lost its significance. Baptism reflects the Exodus experience by which the people of God go from slavery to freedom, from death to life. It is the entry into a new life, a new land, a new age, a very different time that did not exist before. Incorporated into the body of Christ we are brought into a new community, a new order of life, a new creation. It points to the ultimate renewal of the world. It is the symbol of our incorporation into the whole new body of humanity, and of a life of freedom.

With this understanding, youth also disputed the meaning of the theology and practice of confirmation. What does the rite celebrating the beginning of full membership in the church imply? Traditional automatic confirmation ignores the spiritual struggle of youth and makes them members of the Christian community without any condition and commitment. Catechetical classes leave them unprepared for the battle against the status quo in the church and the grim divisions in society. Confirmation in the churches is an introverted and individualistic affair. It obscures the dynamic function of the Christian community and glosses over the manifold complexities of the world. The institutional church provides answers only to the religious and moral questions of the past instead of fostering a spirit of free enquiry leading to personal and corporate decision-making.

Slowly, through these debates and controversies, the very concept of the integration of youth in the church was challenged. Integration within the existing ecclesiastical structures is only an invitation to conform. No possibility is offered to youth to be at the same time relatively distant from and deeply involved in the Christian community in order that they become critical participants in it. Integration appeared like a species of domestication calculated to ensure that youth had no part in the thinking and policy-making process.

Not only did integration become a suspect word; the term leadership, so readily accepted during earlier periods of youth work, was subjected to critical examination. The educators of youth are older people and behave like older people. Youth movements succeed when they are turned into adult-led youth organizations. Leadership training is more important than youth service itself since youth leaders become effective only as the confidants of young people. Educators are to be held up as superb (middle-class) examples for the young generation. The whole of urban youth is to be made into an educated class. If loss of authority is admitted, the adult empire would totter. Stability more than flexibility, knowledge more than inquiry, predictability more than trustworthiness, proclaiming rather than listening are considered to be the dominant traits of youth leaders. Thus adolescents are trained not to rebel against the older generation.

The conflict between generations

The crisis in ecumenical youth work came to a head in the early sixties. A widespread underground movement, ignored for the most part by the majority of experienced church leaders, now came to the surface. Both the Ecumenical Youth Assembly at Lausanne and the World Teaching Conference at Strasbourg in 1960 inaugurated a new period of rapid and radical change. Youth became increasingly caught up in its own agonies, dilemmas and aspirations. Forced into restless encounters with Christian and secular communities it searched on its own for meaning in the gospel of reconciliation. A sense of discipline and responsibility was to be recovered through independent participation in the mission of the church and its service to the world.

Throughout the sixties young people were destined to press too hard for solutions and to overshoot the marks, as they underestimated the influence of tradition and prejudice in the churches and the innumerable complexities of an emerging interdependent world society. The confidence of previous generations in the possibility of finding "Christian solutions to human problems" left them unprepared to face their own emotional simplicity and intellectual inadequacy. It is heart-warming to note that the youth, convinced that the love of God should find expression through human beings in caring community and social reform, openly admitted on several occasions that it lacked the expertise to analyze socio-political problems and complex economic issues. It was often at a loss when it participated in adult and expert deliberations.

To tell the story of the politicization of youth, including youth in the World Council of Churches, is not an easy task. In an exploratory examination of such a large topic there are bound to be gaps and questions. Politicization is marked by two features: awareness and engagement. Not only did it dawn upon young men and women that an intimate connection exists between the religious and socio-political areas of life; youth had also to become vocal and active in the human affairs of the *polis*. Step by step, from the geographical region, to the nation, the continent, the hemisphere and the world, youth searched out the formative processes which create reality, and moved from observer to participant, from a passive to an active phase. Powerless and voiceless in the past, the young generation pushed hard to be inserted into the major institutions that affect young people's life.

Particularly in the realm of education, youth protested that adults had assumed voicelessness and powerlessness as a normal condition of the young. Schools had in the past a custodial style largely because they were seen as custodial institutions by much of the general public. Their "hidden curriculum" served to foster passivity and submission. Now a confrontation between teacher and student was called for. Students must have a place in working out with their teachers an agreement about their mutual enterprise, in which disputation and disagreement play a larger role, in order that institutions of learning can deal appropriately with the engagement dimension of politicization.

Youth applied similar criteria to institutions of religious education. They should offer far greater opportunity for growth in self-direction and leadership, establishing a climate of dialogue within which the Christian points of view could be confronted, clarified, judged, and revised. Too large a claim, however, was made, in hoping that religious educators would have a decisive influence where religious and political awareness intersect.

The problematic of the politicization of youth was very visible at the Uppsala Assembly in 1968. The high degree of consciousness and the intensity of engagement were beyond dispute. Young people had developed on their own new methods of involvement to hammer home the urgency of common service to the suffering, the exploited and the poor. The sharing of the bread in the eucharist, they felt, must be directly related to the pursuit of international justice. The divisions of the churches aggravate human conflicts and the struggles in the world perpetuate the polarization of the churches. The gulf between the affluent and the destitute cuts across all denominational and confessional lines. The imprisonment in a false Christian anthropology, it was instinctively felt, is the root cause of the churches' inability to denounce the paternalistic and imperialist attitudes of the developed countries towards the underdeveloped nations.

Nevertheless, the youth participants in the Assembly were as vulnerable as the adult delegates. In spite of their effective new style of communication, their recommendations and proposals were not more to the purpose than the official decisions of the world gathering. They only grasped imperfectly that identification with the victims of racial discrimination, economic and ideological oppression involved more than the staging of demonstrations and the shouting of slogans. Too few of the youth participants were a visible part of the crying misery and the desperate predicament of the oppressed millions. The challenges and implications of the development decade were not squarely faced. Both the old and the young generation could not anticipate that in the years ahead the rich would become still richer, and the poor still poorer. Within a short time an even greater escalation in the arms race and an unexpected world oil crisis would hasten that process.

The present era

The present era has been marked by even more far-reaching changes and unforseeable developments in the orientation, behaviour and commitment of youth. In chapter 7 reference was made to the new situation made up of neo-conservatives, a silent, uninvolved majority, a confused and searching sector, and a minority of socio-political activists. The World Council and its member churches were confronted with the necessity of recognizing the plurality of new advances and dispositions of young people in the North and the South, and the East and the West. The counter-cultures and new religions of youth, which had started earlier, were in full swing. The need for a critical analysis of these phenomena from sociological and psychological perspectives was apparent. But there was little sense of urgency.

Several reasons can be given for this hesitation and failure. From 1970 onwards a considerable number of new ecumenical programmes and concerns were added to the existing ones, such as dialogue with people of living faiths; ecumenical education; health, healing and wholeness; the programme to combat racism; the churches' participation in development; the battle against the violation of human rights; the issue of the human control of science and technology in an unjust world; the church in solidarity with the poor. The recently issued *Instruction on Certain Aspects of the Theology of Liberation*, issued by the Sacred Congregation for the Doctrine of Faith, contains this revealing passage: "We should recall that the preferential option described at *Puebla* (the General Conference of the Latin American episcopate in 1979) is twofold: for the poor and *for the young*. It is significant that the option for the young has in general been passed over in total silence."[5] Indeed, the role of youth in the practice of liberation theology was not spelled out. In the World Council of Churches also that option was passed over.

Besides being involved in a greater number of ecumenical programmes, the Council had to deal with a variety of indigenous ecumenical developments in many regions of the world. The Council's youth office, just as the WSCF, struggled with the problems of a right balance between centralization and decentralization, the attention to be paid to overall as against specific ecumenical concerns, and the gap in communication between the international headquarters in Geneva and the different youth networks and constituencies throughout the world. Many national and regional youth organizations were satisfied with their particular achievements and resisted interference in their internal affairs. The task of sorting out areas of cooperation and areas of friction became more complicated.

Plans to hold a world youth conference in 1981 did not materialize. The YMCA, the YWCA and the WSCF felt threatened by the prospect of such a major event. The YMCA argued that it had full Roman Catholic participation and could not take part in a world conference unless there was full Catholic involvement. The WSCF was still sorting out its domestic problems and was seriously short of funds. Regional and national youth organizations also resisted what they saw as the paternalistic attitude of the WCC in taking the initiative and setting the agenda for a world gathering. They criticized the World Council for its alleged bureaucratic strangling of the ecumenical movement. There was clearly a lack of international communication and cooperation.

Yet, not surprisingly, the Council insisted that an ever more adequate representation of young people on the staff, programmes, commissions and decision-making bodies had to be pursued. A reasonable presence of young people at assemblies and other major world conferences and their involvement at all levels of the planning and decision-making process had to be achieved. There is no doubt that the Sub-unit on Youth has been quite successful in promoting the important role of stewards at the last two Assemblies and meetings of the Central Committee. But in the process, it has become an almost purely functional entity of the Council without its own specific programme of substance and quality. The Sub-unit on Youth had to admit that "it must find ways to enable youth in greater numbers to contribute *their insights* to the ecumenical movement. Much more work needs to be done to ensure participation by young people in *responsible positions* within the WCC."[6]

The insistence on better official youth representation was finally but a diversion and reflected the failure of the Council and its member churches to engage in a critical analysis and evaluation, from all angles, of counter-cultures and the new religions of youth, and of ecological and peace movements. As Christian communities neglected to examine the cultural and ideological factors of their own existence, particularly in relation to the predicament and the behaviour of the young generation, they were unable to raise the question, in a radical way, of the future of youth.

Counter-cultures and new religions

The counter-cultures of the young have posed a fundamental challenge to the Western cultural tradition. Profoundly alienated from adult church and adult society, youth went its own way, leaving it to adults to tackle the world's problems. The older generation itself clung to its traditional attitude, since the youth searching for new norms, values, social structures and life-styles was apparently a small proportion of the total youth population. Facile generalizations, instead of a careful assessment of contemporary youth, were deemed sufficient in view of the transient and limited character of the deviation and dissent. Also the assumption that the counter-cultures had a worldly orientation and were militantly secular, added to the reservations of the church hierarchy. In actual fact they were, with a few exceptions, deeply religious, though not in the sense in which evangelical church leaders would define religion. Their quest for the sacred was an odd amalgam of the Eastern and the Western, yet another sign of how deeply alienated from the immediate cultural traditions the counter-cultures were.

The variety of religious communities — the Divine Light Mission, Hare Krishna, Bhagwan Shree Rajneesh, Ananda Marga, the Unification Church, the Process Church of the Final Judgment, scientology, the Jesus People and the Children of God — represented attempts to establish religious communities as alternatives to established churches. All these communities continue to reject in one way or another the values of the establishment — income or education, status distinctions based on occupational prestige, worship of technological achievement, the apparent lack of honesty in human relations, the gap between professed values and actions.

The problem, however, remains whether youth cultures and newly blended religions are indeed capable of embodying viable alternative communities. The "sacred" can be either holy or demonic, and it is not always easy to distinguish the one from the other. Insofar as members of counter-cultures strove to achieve meaning, mystery and one-ness through the replacement of institutional structures by their various versions of fellowship, they have tended to remain unrealistic and irresponsible. Insofar, however, as they keep alive their personalistic, intuitive and experimental communalism as a dialectical element in the traditional church and in modern society, they are, for all their differences, playing a crucial role in the task of making human life more fulfillingly human.

The period of the counter-culture has already been superseded by a new period of "counter-counter-culture". The majority of youth has become inarticulate, visionless and uninvolved. It prefers to be down-to-earth, sedate, modest and without illusions. It is weary of all social and political action because in its opinion conflicts and strife in society will continue without leading to tangible results. It is not worthwhile to sacrifice one's life for the survival of the nation. There is no cure for the various forms of ugly racism. Socialist and communist ideologies have failed. Class struggle is an invention of outdated revolutionaries. The capitalist system has not performed any better and is also in need of far-reaching change. The effects of worldwide unemployment will become increasingly disastrous. The only choice is a retreat into a personal environment which provides limited meaning and satisfaction.

Some recent polls in fact indicate that narrow kinship relations are most highly valued by the young generation. More than 80 percent have confidence in their parents and are not eager to leave early the family cell

— a radical change in attitude from what it was twenty years ago. More than 50 percent is anxious to cultivate close bonds with brothers, sisters and friends. On the other hand, very few youth want to extend their own family beyond two children. Trust in clergy, teachers, employers and public servants is often dismally low. Friendship, work, scientific progress, income, travel, sports, arts, sexuality — in this order — are rated much higher than patriotism, religion, revolution, military service and politics — in that order.

According to a poll carried out by the *Figaro-Magazine* in March 1984 in France, only 7 percent of Roman Catholic youth between 16 and 22 profess that they regularly practise their religion, 12 percent practise it occasionally, and 48 percent not at all. Four per cent adhere to other religions and 29 percent are without religion. The freedom to fashion one's own life is deemed essential. Before one starts believing in God, one must believe in oneself. Honesty in life, moral integrity and a moderate dose of altruism are prerequisites for an authentic practice of religion. The expression of faith, however, is a hazardous affair and seldom necessary. Some experts might question these statistics and conclusions. But one thing is sure: a silent and uninvolved majority of youth live today on the fringe of society and outside the confines of the established church more than ever before.

Ecological movements

There is a minority of young socio-political activists, passionately engaged in movements for the preservation of nature and for lasting harmony and peace in the world. Ecological pressure groups vary in their character from country to country. In some Western nations they are well organized as political parties. There are also ecological movements of young people in the third world. Teach-ins, letter-writing campaigns, electoral and parliamentary politics, protest marches and occupation of sites of polluting industries and nuclear power plants are among the means adopted by "the green" revolutionaries. Needless to say, ecology and counter-culture religion have close interconnections. Given the fact that Western culture has arrived at an amoral, anti-nature, blindly mechanistic technocracy, the ecological attitude is truly counter-cultural. But it is at the same time religious. The ecological crisis will not be solved until a sense of the spiritual affinity between human beings and their environment is recaptured. Youth strikes at the heart of the ideological foundations of the Atlantic community which have led to a faith in the ever greater advance of science and technology. The Judeo-Christian tradition has played an important part in fostering that process. Now a

transformation of conscience is urgently required because the environmental collapse, in its broadest meaning, is a religious failure, demanding
a change in the most fundamental beliefs and attitudes.

Many young people feel that the degrading and disastrous results of an
excessive anthropocentrism in the Christian religion can be corrected by
listening to the wisdom of Eastern religions which conceive nature not as
a dead, material thing to be exploited, but as a self-contained entity, with
an integrity of being in and of itself. It is not a thing for human use and
conquest but a being to be enjoyed and admired. Human beings and
nature share a mutual reciprocity which presupposes a fundamental
identity between the two. There is no dichotomy between the human
species as the possessor and nature as the possessed; rather the human
species is a participant in the natural cosmos. Nature is a teacher, not
through the noise of words, but through the sound of silence, not through
reason, but through feeling. If this insight is not recovered the "eco-
catastrophe" will be unavoidable.

Peace movements

Similarly, the ultimate goal of the active involvement of youth in peace
movements today is the prevention of the irreparable destruction of our
planet. Young generations have supported numerous pacifist groups
throughout this century. Their radical anti-war activism has greatly
increased during the last few decades. Particularly European youth has
known the futility of the reliance on force.

There are numerous peace movements of young people in many
countries of the first world; but those in the Netherlands and the Federal
Republic of Germany are the strongest and the most outspoken. The
Evangelical Kirchentag, held in June 1981 in Hamburg, centred on the
theme "Fear Not", and brought together 125,000 people, 60 percent of
whom were under 25. The four-day event gave expression to the peace
concerns so deeply felt among youth in West Germany. In the same year
thousands of young people marched in a huge peace demonstration in
Amsterdam criticizing the "balance of terror" and protesting against the
stationing of cruise missiles on Dutch soil. A similar massive demonstration took place in Bonn. Many other recent peace rallies could be
mentioned. The majority of the young peace activists are without church
affiliation; many young people participating in the Kirchentag reject the
established church.

Although the peace movements in Western Europe are less ideological
today than in the sixties (when young leftists struggled to find their
identity), more attracted to non-violence, less marked by intergenera-

tional hostility and more inclusive of the working class, they still are in danger of being manipulated by internationally controlled aggressive and subversive forces. New political groups have emerged in the Federal Republic of Germany, such as the Alternatives — anti-nuclear reactor activists and young people seeking a new life-style as well as total military disarmament — and the Green Party, which is concerned with environmental issues. To the surprise of many, the Alternatives and the Greens have been siphoning off more than 7 percent of the vote from the traditional parties — the Social Democrats, the Free Democrats and the Christian Democrats. New groups keep springing up within the peace movement. The peace advocacy of the young in several nations is strengthened as they learn from each other's witness.

Power, culture, dialogue, spirituality

This panorama of cool, dedicated, indifferent, searching and restless youth shows the recent shortcomings and failures of the World Council of Churches in the realm of its youth activities. Ecumenical leaders have not taken the trouble to compare the political youth of the sixties with the a-political youth of the eighties and to arrive at some obvious conclusions. Youth at the Uppsala Assembly were deeply inspired by the prophets of the Old Testament — and the contemporary prophetic voices. It staged a powerful play "On That Day", by Olov Hartman, based on the cry for justice and the prophecy of doom in the Book of Amos. At the end of the striking performance the lights went out in the plenary hall and the youth, having left the stage, shouted from the corridors "Prepare to meet your God". There was a stony silence for several minutes. The delegates were stunned and at a loss.

Youth in our decade is inspired and stirred by the Jesus of the Beatitudes and by that strange crowd of people who have a gentle spirit, whose hearts are pure and who are called to be peace-makers. The present peace movements of Christian young people have their origin in the non-violent Jesus, even when they are obviously obscured by the disruptive activities of anti-religious youth. Christian youth of the sixties was "progressively left"; Christian youth today is "progressively right".

The World Council of Churches and its entire constituency, therefore, should not miss the opportunity to express the hope that Christian youth is again at the threshold of unexpected new ways of concerted action and exploration. The clear-sightedness and the keen sense of hearing of both the old and the young generation have to be newly tested. *New* ecumenical structures of communication, learning and sharing need to be devised in order that youth makes *its* contribution to *new* ecumenical adventures.

As youth has become both more versatile and more circumspect today than twenty years ago, it needs to be encouraged to express itself more explicitly on such issues as power, culture, dialogue and spirituality. Since the Vancouver Assembly in 1983 these issues are high on the agenda of the World Council.

Young people, more than the adult generation, are deeply aware of and opposed to the increasing intransigence, irrationality and inhumanness of concentrated political, economic, technological and military power which undergirds the doctrine of national security. This power becomes still more demonic when it is justified through fanatical ideological and religious convictions. The myth of national superiority does not guarantee the security of people; it dehumanizes social relations and perverts authentic manifestations of life. Youth is in the forefront of the attempts to build up people's power designed to shape a more participatory society through the legitimate exercise of power. It experiences that the lives of the poor and the marginalized, considered disposable by the powerful, are in fact of infinite value, because they are God's gift.

Young people, even more than the old generation, squarely face the sad reality that churches themselves often support or tolerate oppression and domination. In too many instances church life merely reflects its social environment; society's weakest members have no part in leadership roles and decision-making processes. The powers of ecclesiastical institutions, so far only partly demythologized, need to be further exposed and resisted. God chose what is foolish in the world to shame the strong (1 Cor. 1:27). Many young people insist that it is not only necessary to repeat these words, but to find out what this means in terms of power. How for the sake of a new church and a new humanity may the powerless exercise power? Christian youth instinctively searches and yearns for a power which absorbs "powerful power" rather than counters power with power. If any creative human society is to be built, it is literally necessary to love one's enemies in class struggles, revolutions and schisms.

Many young people live in the plural wonder of cultures and realize that listening to and receiving from receptor cultures is an essential part of testifying to God's salvation of the world. They are anxious to experience the rich variety of the manifestations of the Christian faith which are a transforming power in the life of different communities. They are concerned that the emergence of Christian communities within minority groups that affirm their cultural identity is not stamped out simply because they are seen as a threat to the dominant culture. Many young Christians joyfully acknowledge that Christ both judges and transcends Western confessionalism and denominationalism in their cultural settings.

The three historical divisions in Western Christianity — Orthodoxy, Roman Catholicism and Protestantism — are not justified in assuming that they exclusively constitute *the* church. There are obviously different historical, cultural and sociological influences at work.

Young disciples of Christ have begun to glimpse that the possibilities and implications of cultural diversity have to be taken seriously in the context of the ecumenical activity of God. The creative indigenous resources for understanding the gospel afresh are not to be found in any one ecclesiastical centre — Rome, Geneva, Wittenberg, Constantinople, Moscow — but throughout the world. Increasingly young adults experience that any culture is, above all, a culture of *people*. A theology which deals more with abstract concepts than with the life of people is not equipped to grasp the relations between the gospel and culture. The incarnate Christ is neither above culture, nor opposed to culture; nor does he simply transform culture. He lives with and in peoples' cultures as he manifests his redemptive love in all their misery and wellbeing.

In the realm of what we now call "dialogue with people of other living faiths", many young people are much less conditioned by the past than the older generations. They experience in various ways that dialogue is a progressive and cumulative process, which does not only take place through verbal communication, but through the dynamic contact of life with life. Youth can contribute significantly to the appreciation of dialogue as a Christian vocation. While affirming the uniqueness of the life, death and resurrection of Jesus, youth recognizes God's creative and redeeming work, not only in the seeking, but also in the non-cerebral experience of religious truth among people of other faiths.

Worship is central to all renewal in the church. From it visions of young and old Christians are born, and their hopes stirred. In it the failures of the younger and older disciples of Christ are confessed and their schemes, programmes and endeavours offered to God for refinement and transformation. Youth has become very sensitive to renewal in worship and is keen to explore new forms through which Christian spirituality is manifested, as for example, in the struggle for justice and human dignity. The search for and sharing in an authentic spirituality is vital for the moral and political life of the congregation. The liturgical practice of faith and an uncompromising conduct of life are intimately related. Here too the church is yet to benefit from what youth can contribute.

Future outlook

The issues raised here have bearings on the present and future *raison d'être* of the World Council of Churches. And these issues are closely related to the problem of the succession of generations. Does the story of Christian youth during half a century reflect the changes in the ecumenical movement itself? Should the adult generation stick to its careful position on a not too fluid relation between the church and the world because the young generation not only continues to extend the frontiers of the church but even does not hesitate to relate to the multi-religious and secular world? Will the Basis of the World Council of Churches, which speaks of a fellowship of churches that confess Jesus Christ as Lord and Saviour, and its inherent ecclesiological significance have to be watered down in order to meet the anti-establishment and anti-official religious mood of Christian youth?

It is precisely this traditional and careful reasoning which fails to shed new light on the complicated and untransparent predicament of youth. It in fact reflects a nostalgia for earlier certainties in the ecumenical movement. The argument limits the category of "promising" Christian youth to stewards and young delegates in official ecumenical gatherings and to young people still confidently active in their denominations on national and local levels. It gravely overlooks that unclassifiable minority of Christian youth that has become very sensitive to the dire need of a *renewable* church in the midst of a *renewable* human community.

The overall theme of "The Unity of the Church and the Renewal of Human Community" has been on the agenda of the World Council for over fifteen years, but hardly any progress has been made during this time in relating the two dynamically to each other. Until now, the world (God's creation) and humanity (God's people) have not truly and naturally come into the Christian picture. Even today the ecumenical movement finds it difficult to bring itself to admit that the divisions and conflicts in the churches mirror to a great extent the divisions and conflicts in the world. As I have argued, many young Christians have sensed that without repeated confession of failure and deep inner renewal the church cannot become the sacrament of God's plan of salvation to unite all things in Christ as the Lord of a new humanity and a new creation. If the unity of the church is not unconditionally linked to the quality of a new human community in Christ, the church only continues to manifest a pseudo-unity. The consequences of faithfulness to the gospel are far more dramatic than generations of Christians thought they were.

Youth can demonstrate in its own life new ways of faith and witness that the potential unity of the world, in the midst of its divisions and brokenness, and the urgent renewal of the church are part of the same goal of God's universal salvation. It needs youthful insight and courage to stress that the sacramental church is but a function of the human community until the kingdom of God arrives. Baptism, eucharist and ministry are meaningful and effective only within the conflicts of racism, classism and sexism. They heal "the manifold divisions on account of human pride, material interest and power politics... restore human personality and dignity... and above all" blot out "the obstinancy of unjustifiable confessional oppositions within the body of Christ".[7]

As the household of God, of which youth is an integral part and may become once again the *avant garde*, the church of Jesus Christ can be a sign to an evolving society only if it is first and last a true sign of God's judgment and reconciliation. Because Christian youth has come a long way in the ecumenical movement it refuses to state today that "the church is bold in speaking of itself as the sign of the coming unity of mankind".

Through this deliberate and consistent refusal youth incorporates the hope that Christianity is on its way to practise "a new openness to the world in its aspirations, its achievements, its restlessness and despair". This hope is even more justified because youth does have a first-hand experience and is not suspicious or envious that "secular society has produced instruments of conciliation and unification which often seem more effective than the church itself".[8] These quotations are all taken from the report of the Fourth Assembly at Uppsala in 1968, the year youth had a mountain-top vision.

Some readers of this final chapter may argue that I have not taken seriously enough the prolonged alienation and isolation of youth, that since the large minority of young people continue to live on the fringe of — if not outside — the church, artificial efforts to win them back into the fold will have little chance of success.

But I am convinced that new insights into the options of powerlessness (not the options of counter-power), into the plurality (not the domination) of cultures, into the equality (not the hierarchy) of spiritualities, into the privilege (not the duty) of dialogue can only be gained by the old generation and the new generation together. The problem of unity as dynamic conciliarity and reconciled diversity needs to be solved by all Christians, young and old, together. It is high time, therefore, that the Council's Sub-unit on Youth and its constituency stop their domestic deliberations and come into contact with Christian youth beyond official and semi-official boundaries.

It is true that adult Christians tend to escape from the present into defensive justifications of the past. And young Christians tend to escape from the past into utopian projections of the future. Both risk ignoring the quality of newness which the present always possesses, and which changes the understanding of both as to where they came from and where they are to go. They both, therefore, are called to catch a few glimpses of the wholeness of the oikoumene. Their new visions incorporating the inexhaustible truth of the past will then come closer to that unfathomable wholeness of the triune God.

NOTES

[1] *The Ecumenical Youth Commission of the World Alliance for International Friendship through the Churches and the Universal Christian Council for Life and Work*, Geneva, 1936, p.4.

[2] "From Amsterdam to Oslo", in *Christianity as a Youth Movement*, compiled by R.H. Edwin Espy for *Highroad* (Methodist Youth Journal of Religion), Oslo conference edition by courtesy of the Methodist Publishing House, 1947, p.61.

[3] *First Assembly of the World Council of Churches*, ed. W.A. Visser 't Hooft, London, SCM Press, 1949, pp.187-88.

[4] *Minutes and Reports*, Geneva, WCC, 1951, pp.65, 75-78.

[5] London, Catholic Truth Society, 1984, p.16.

[6] *Nairobi to Vancouver, 1975-1983*, Geneva, WCC, 1983, p.213.

[7] *Baptism, Eucharist and Ministry*, Geneva, WCC, 1982, Faith and Order Paper No. 111, p.14.

[8] *The Uppsala Report, 1968*, ed. Norman Goodall, Geneva, WCC, 1968, p.17.

Appendix I: Bibliography

Official publications

Youth and the Church, report to the Continuation Committee of the Stockholm Conference on Life and Work by its youth commission, eds Basil Mathews, Lucy Gardner and Erich Stange. London, Pilgrim Press, 1928, 132pp.

Jugend und Kirche. Denkschrift der Jugendkommission des Fortsetzungsausschusses der Weltkonferenz für praktisches Christentum, vorgelegt bei der Tagung des Fortsetzungsausschusses in Prag, September 1982. Deutsche Ausgabe herausgegeben von Erich Stange. Dresden, Ludwig Ungelenk, 1928, 83pp.

Jeunesses orthodoxes. Genève: Editions de la Commission de jeunesse du Conseil oecuménique du christianisme pratique, 1931, 137pp.

Ricoeur, P.: Conférence internationale de la jeunesse à Gland (Suisse), 29 août-4 septembre 1933. Reprinted from: *Christianisme social*, 1933, 7pp.

The Ecumenical Youth Commission of the World Alliance for International Friendship through the Churches and the Universal Christian Council for Life and Work. Geneva, 1936, 8pp. French: *La foi qui triomphe du monde*.

World Christian Youth Commission. Geneva, 1949, 31pp. Also: Geneva, 1950, 16pp.

Amsterdam, 1939

Amsterdam — What Next? London: Council of the Churches on the Christian Faith and the Common Life, Commission on International Friendship and Social Responsibility, 48pp.

"Can You Still Say 'Christus Victor'?" A symposium in commemoration of the First World Conference of Christian Youth, ed. R.H. Edwin Espy, introduction by W.A. Visser 't Hooft. In *Journal of Ecumenical Studies*, special issue, Vol. 16, No. 1, winter 1979.

Christus Victor. The report of the World Conference of Christian Youth, Amsterdam, 24 July-2 August 1939. Geneva, Conference headquarters, 1939, 252pp. Also in French, German and Spanish.

Christus Victor. World Conference of Christian Youth, services of worship, 11 pamphlets.

Christus Victor. Worship at the conference, 35pp. Also in French.

Further Studies on the Christian Community in the Modern World. Second preparatory study outline for the World Conference of Christian Youth. Geneva, Conference headquarters, 1939, 123pp. French: *Nouvelle série d'études...*; German: *Weitere Studien...*

Gethman, Walter W. and Denzil G.M. Patrick: *The Christian Community in the Modern World*. A preparatory study for the World Conference of Christian Youth. Geneva, Conference headquarters, 1938, 100pp.

Liang, C.C.: *English Edition of the Reports of the Chinese Delegates to the World Conference of Christian Youth*. Shanghai, The China-Amsterdam Committee, 1939, 57pp.

Ouellette, Edward F.: *Can You Say Christus Victor?* A study outline based on the World Conference of Christian Youth. New York, Universal Christian Council, 1939, 56pp.

Report of the Canadian Delegation to the World Conference of Christian Youth. Toronto, Canadian-Amsterdam Committee, 1939, 36pp.

Visser 't Hooft, W.A. and Suzanne de Dietrich: *The Faith Which Overcomes the World*. Bible studies compiled at the request of the Executive Committee of the Amsterdam World Christian Youth Conference. London, Student Christian Movement Press, 1940, 31pp.

We Remember Amsterdam 1939-1979: Christus Victor, Forty Years after the First World Conference of Christian Youth. Contributors: W.A. Visser 't Hooft, J.J. von Allmen, Madeleine Barot, and others, 1979, mimeographed.

Oslo 1947

Can the Churches Work Together? A study outline for youth groups based on Christian witness in the post-war world. London, British Council of Churches, 1947, 32pp.

The Chief Speeches at Oslo. Addresses at the World Christian Youth Conference, Oslo, July 1947. Madras, Christian Literature Society, 1947, 33pp.

Conference Handbook. Guide pour la conférence. Konferenz-Handbuch. Oslo, World Conference of Christian Youth, 1947, 81pp.

Dietrich, Suzanne de: *Bible Study Outlines*. World Conference of Christian Youth, Oslo, July 1947. Geneva, La Tribune de Genève, 1947, 10pp.

Espy, R.H. Edwin, ed.: *Christianity as a Youth Movement*. Compiled for *Highroad*, Methodist Youth Journal of Religion. Oslo conference edition, Methodist Publishing House, 1947, 64pp.

Ferguson, Rowena: *Christian Youth in the United States of America*. The United States Planning Committee, 1947, 27pp.

Jesus Christ is Lord. Services of worship, 9 pamphlets.

Preliminary Questions (Ten questions and a supplementary booklet). Geneva, La Tribune de Genève, 1947. French: *Questions préliminaires*. German: *Fragen zur Vorbereitung*.

The Report of the Second World Conference of Christian Youth, Oslo, Norway, 22-31 July 1947, ed. Paul Griswold Macy. Geneva, WCC, 1947, 256pp. French: *Rapport de la deuxième conférence mondiale de la jeunesse chrétienne*. German: *Bericht über die Zweite Weltkonferenz christlicher Jugend*. Spanish: Jesucristo es el Señor.

Small, Mabel and Norman J. Bull: *Oslo Calling: the Story of the Second World Conference of Christian Youth*. Wallington, Religious Education Press, 1947, 93pp.

Tomkins, Oliver: *Youth in the World-Church*. A preparatory study for the Second World Conference of Christian Youth, Oslo, July 1947. Geneva, La Tribune de Genève, 1947, 28pp. German: *Jugend und Weltkirche*.

Urgente Vragen Over Jeugd, Kerk en Maatschappij. Amsterdam, W. ten Have, 1947, 88pp.

World Conference of Christian Youth: List of Delegates. Oslo, 22-31 July 1947, 50pp.

Travancore, 1952

Footprints in Travancore. Report of the Third World Conference of Christian Youth, 11-26 December 1952. Coonoor, Nilgiris, India Sunday School Union, 1953, 95pp.

World Conference of Christian Youth, Travancore, India, December 1952. *Workbook*. Geneva, World Alliance of YMCAs, 50pp.

Lausanne 1960

Ecumenical Youth Assembly in Europe, Booklet. Ökumenische Jugendkonferenz in Europa, Büchlein. Assemblée oecuménique de la jeunesse européenne, Livret. Lausanne, 1960, 112pp.

Ecumenical Youth Assembly in Europe, Delegates. Ökumenische Jugendkonferenz in Europa, Delegierte. Assemblée oecuménique de la jeunesse européenne, delegués. Lausanne, 1960, 32pp.

Ecumenical Youth Assembly in Europe, Groupleaders Booklet. Assemblée oecuménique de la jeunesse européenne, Livret des chefs de groupe. Ökumenische Jugendkonferenz in Europa, Heft für Gruppenleiter. Lausanne, 1960, 24pp.

Ecumenical Youth Assembly in Europe, Lausanne, 1960. *Now What?*, 20pp. Also in French and German.

Ecumenical Youth Assembly in Europe, Lausanne, July 1960. *Preparatory Studies*, 50pp., mimeographed. Also in Dutch, Finnish, French, German, Greek, Italian, Spanish, Swedish.

French, Rod, ed.: *Ecumenical Youth Assembly in Europe, Lausanne, 1960*. Geneva, WCC Youth Department, 1960, 91pp. (*Youth*, No. 2, October 1960).

Veni Creator Spiritus, worship booklet, Ecumenical Youth Assembly in Europe, 1960. Taizé, Les Presses de Taizé, 1960, 284pp. Also in French and German.

Ann Arbor, 1961

North American Youth Assembly, Ann Arbor, 1961, ed. Rod French. Geneva, WCC Youth Department, 1961, 50pp. (*Youth*, No. 4, November 1961).

Nairobi, 1962-1963

All Africa Christian Youth Assembly, *Bible Studies: Freedom Under the Cross*. Nairobi, 28 December 1962-7 January 1963. Geneva, World Student Christian Federation, 1962, 30pp. Also in French.

Assemblée de la jeunesse chrétienne de toute l'Afrique, *Manuel de l'Assemblée* — All African Christian Youth Assembly, *Assembly Handbook*, Nairobi, 28 December-7 January, 1963, 24pp.

What Is It To Us? Freedom under the Cross. Quotations and questions from the All Africa Christian Youth Assembly, Nairobi, 28 December, 1962-7 January 1963. Published for the Assembly Planning Committee. Geneva, World Student Christian Federation, 1963, 43pp. Also in French.

Dumaguete City, Philippines, 1964-1965

Asian Christian Youth Assembly. *The Directory of Asian Christian Youth Assembly Participants, 1965*. Bangkok, S. Hongladaromp-Printer and Publisher, 1966, 55pp.

Christ the Life. The report of the Asian Christian Youth Assembly, Silliman University, Dumaguete City 1964-1965. Part One: Lectures, biblical messages, sermons, ed. Soritua A.E. Nababan, 130pp.

Other official publications

Christian Youth in a Troubled Society. Ayia Napa, Cyprus, 13-20 July 1978. Geneva, Middle East Council of Churches Youth Programme, 1978, 75pp.

Congregemur: "Let Us Come Together", a worship booklet for modern young people. Geneva, WCC, 1965, 63pp. Revised version 1967. Also in French and German.

Consultation of Christian Youth Leaders, Beirut, Lebanon, 18-26 April 1955. Geneva, WCC Youth Department, 1955, 75pp.

Ecumenical Commitment and Christian Education. A report to the WCC Commission on Faith and Order, the World Council of Christian Education and the WCC Youth Department. Geneva, WCC, 1968, 40pp.

First Inter-regional Ecumenical Youth Encounter: Human Rights, Peoples' Rights: Panama, August 1980. Berlin, Ecumenical Youth Council in Europe, 1981, 92pp. Text in English, French and German.

Lasset uns beten: Gebete im Aufbaulager — Let Us Pray: a work camper's book of worship — Prions: un livre de prière pour les camps de travail. Geneva, WCC Youth Department, 1952, 64pp.

One Lord, One World. Report of the Third (New Zealand) Ecumenical Youth Conference, Lower Hutt, 27 December 1960-4 January 1961. Christchurch, H.F. Cross, 1961, 64pp.

Pacific Conference of Churches. *The Dancing Convention: Youths of the 80s*. Suva, Fiji, Lotu Pasifika Productions, 1980, 45pp.

The New Creation and the New Generation: a Forum for Youth Workers, ed. Albert van den Heuvel. New York, Friendship Press, 1965, 127pp.

Songs, Hymns and Liturgies for the International Youth Consultation "Stift Urach", Stuttgart, 24-31 July 1981, 43pp.

Travail de jeunesse. Traduction française d'articles parus dans le numéro de janvier 1963, vol. XV, no. 2 de *The Ecumenical Review*, Geneva, WCC, 1963, 40pp.

Tremewan, Chris: *Teatime at the Revolution*. Hong Kong, World Student Christian Federation, Asia-Pacific Region, 1983, WSCF Asia-Pacific Book, 8, 145pp.

We Shall All Unite! Report of the Fourth Ecumenical Youth Conference, Hamilton, New Zealand. Christchurch, National Council of Churches, 1966, 75pp.

When We Share, ed. Frances Maeda. New York, Friendship Press, 1957, 64pp.

When We Work Together, ed. William A. Perkins. New York, Friendship Press, 1960, 64pp.

World Study of Church Youth Work. A summary of information and judgments concerning youth work of the churches. London, New York, World Council of Christian Education and Sunday School Association, 1951, 106pp., mimeographed.

Youth and the Church. Report to the Continuation Committee of the Stockholm Conference on Life and Work by its youth commission, eds Basil Mathews, Lucy Gardner and Erich Stange. London, Pilgrim Press, 1928, 132pp.

Serial publications

News Sheet, issued by the Youth Department of the World Council of Churches, October 1947-October 1959 (published six times annually)

Bulletin du Départment de jeunesse: January 1951-October 1955

Youth, Nos 1-10, 1960-1964
No. 1: Youth and Social Change
No. 2: Ecumenical Youth Assembly in Europe
No. 3: Service
No. 4: North American Youth Assembly, Ann Arbor 1961
No. 5: Living Ethics
No. 6: Many Churches, One Table, One Church
No. 7: Wine and Wine-Skins
No. 8: Visible Proclamation — the Church and Drama
No. 9: Ecumenical Handbook
No.10: Youth, Complex Society, Structures of a Missionary Church

Ecumenical Youth News, January 1961-December 1968 (7-10 issues per year)

Occasional Papers from the Youth Department, Nos 1-5, April 1961-February 1964

Feuillets occasionnels du Département de jeunesse, nos 1-5, April 1961-February 1964

Risk, Vols 1-13, 1965-1977
Vol. 1, No. 1: Gospel for Atheists
Vol. 1, No. 2: The Ordained Ministry
Vol. 1, Nos 3 and 4: The Ministry of Meanings
Vol. 2, No. 1: Christian Education and Ecumenical Commitment
Vol. 2, No. 2: Youth and Revolution
Vol. 2, No. 3: New Hymns for a New Day
Vol. 2, No. 4: Confessional Loyalty at All Costs?
Vol. 3, Nos 1 and 2: The Development Apocalypse (or) Will International Injustice Kill the Ecumenical Movement?

Vol. 3, No. 3: The 95 Theses, 1517-1967
Vol. 3, No. 4: Him Again (The Meaning of the Word of God)
Vol. 4, No. 1: The Negro Church in the USA
Vol. 4, No. 2: Assembly in a Hungry World
Vol. 4, No. 3: Youth in God's World
Vol. 4, No. 4: The Many Voices of Uppsala
Vol. 5, No. 1: Living Liturgical Style
Vol. 5, No. 2: Development Documentation
Vol. 5, Nos 3 and 4: Renewal
Vol. 6, No. 1: Letters from Asia
Vol. 6, No. 2: Good Will or Evil Goods?
Vol. 6, No. 3: Just Men Desert
Vol. 6, No. 4: School or Scandal
Vol. 7, No. 1: Gladly We Rebel
Vol. 7, No. 2: Exalt the Humble
Vol. 7, No. 3: ...And Some Fell on Good Ground
Vol. 7, No. 4: Ways of Life: Ways of Death
Vol. 8, No. 1: ...All Things in Common
Vol. 8, No. 2: De-mythologizing the Dutch
Vol. 8, No. 3: Jacob's Ladder
Vol. 8, No. 4: The New Fishermen
Vol. 9, No. 1: Angry for Peace
Vol. 9, No. 2: Intercommunication — a Symposium on Black Theology
                and Latin American Theology of Liberation
Vol. 9, No. 3: Tell Out My Glory
Vol. 9, No. 4: In Journeyings Often
Vol.10, No. 1: Hope Deferred
Vol.10, No. 2: Words to the Churches — Voices of the Sisters
Vol.10, No. 3: Caught in a Web
Vol.10, No. 4: Ujamaa Safari
Vol.11, No. 1: Pilgrims of the Obvious (Paulo Freire and Ivan Illich)
Vol.11, Nos 2 and 3: A Worship Book for the Fifth Assembly of the World Council of
                Churches
Vol.11, No. 4: Harambee!
Vol.12, No. 1: Song of the Pacific
Vol.12, No. 2: Lift Up Your Hearts
Vol.12, No. 3: Be Thou My Vision — The Cameraman
Vol.13, No. 1: The Silence is Broken
Vol.13, No. 2: No Last Frontier — Dene Nation, the Struggle of Canada's Internal Colony
                for Self-Determination
Vol.13, No. 3: Inside Out — a Style for Dialogue

Youth Newsletter, Youth Sub-unit of the World Council of Churches, 1977- (quarterly)

Jeunesse, Section jeunesse du Conseil oecuménique des Eglises, 1977-

Appendix II: Conferences and Consultations

of the Ecumenical Youth Commission of the World Alliance for International Friendship through the Churches and the Universal Christian Council for Life and Work, 1932-1938, of the WCC Youth Department, 1947-1970, and the WCC Sub-unit on Youth, 1971-

Most conferences and consultations are documented by files in the WCC Youth archives. Only specific mimeographed, offset or printed documents and reports are listed.

Ecumenical Youth Commission of the World Alliance for International Friendship through the Churches and the Universal Council for Life and Work, 1932-1938

Gland, Switzerland, 24-31 August 1932: *Youth Social Study Week.* The world economic and international situation and the message of the Stockholm movement were discussed. Contributions by N. Zernov, A. Philip, D. Bonhoeffer, B. Pickard, P. Toureille, A.A. Paul, M. Lauga. English, French and German discussion groups.

Gland, Switzerland, 29 August-4 September 1933: *International Youth Conference. The Task of the Church in the Social International Crisis.* Contributions by F.W.T. Craske, A. Philip, T. Kilborn, M. Thelin, F. Sohlmann, H.L. Henriod, W.P. Merrill, Bishop of Ripon, P. Ricoeur.

Fanø, Denmark, 22-29 August 1934: *International Youth Conference.* Contributions by D. Bonhoeffer, P. Toureille, F.W.T. Craske, F.N. Zernov.

Chamby, Montreux, Switzerland, 2-8 August 1935: *International Youth Conference. Liberty and Authority.* Contributions by J. Horton, F.W.T. Craske, M. Rucart, F. Siegmund-Schultze, P. Toureille, Mrs Zander.

La Borcarderie, Neuchâtel, Switzerland, 8-14 September 1936: *International Christian Youth Conference.* Contributions by A. Bouvier, F.W.T. Craske, R.H.E. Espy, H.L. Henriod, H. Schönfeld, F. Wartenweiler, I. Winterhager.

Budapest, Hungary, 13-16 November 1936: *Ecumenical Youth Conference of Central European Countries.* Contributions by R.H.E. Espy, A. Bouvier, N. Makay, J. de Ferencz.

Sjöstrand, Norway, 30 August-4 September 1938: *Ecumenical Youth Conference. Youth and Ecumenism in Faith and Action.* Contributions by N. Zernov, R.H.E. Espy, F.W.T. Craske, G. Sparring.

WCC Youth Department 1947-1970

Presinge, Switzerland, October 1947: *First European Youth Planning Conference.* Sponsored jointly by the WCC Youth Department and the WCC Reconstruction Department.

Magliaso, Switzerland, 3-6 April 1948: *European Youth Leaders' Conference.* Contributions by J.M. Fraser, M. Barot, H.A. Visser, U. Smidt.

Presinge, Switzerland, 8-11 November 1948: *Second European Youth Planning Conference*. Contributions by J. Mirejovsky, R. Mackie, W.A. Visser 't Hooft, J. Fraser.

Ecumenical Institute, Bossey, 8-13 January 1949: *Conference of Orthodox Youth*. Contributions by B. Zenkovsky, A. Schmemann, N. Nissiotis, L. Zander, P. Evdokimoff, G. Khodre.

Courteenhall House, England, 21-29 April 1949: *European Youth Leaders' Conference. Christian Freedom and Christian Witness*. The conference took place at the invitation of the youth department of the British Council of Churches.

Presinge, Switzerland, 8-11 November 1949: *Third European Youth Planning Conference*. Contributions by R. Tobias, J. Mirejovsky, G. Booth, Stephen Neill.

Landskron, Villach, Austria, 22-30 April, 1950: *European Youth Leaders' Conference. Evangelization of Youth by Youth*. Contributions by P. Abrecht, H. Gutknecht, J. Joussellin, H. Koch, E.L. Sewell, N. Thompson.

Toronto, Canada, 10-16 August 1950: *Special Conference on Youth Work*. The meeting was held in connection with the World Convention on Christian Education and sponsored by WCCE and the WCC Youth Department. A statement on ecumenical youth work was issued.

Presinge, Switzerland, 6-9 November 1950: *Fourth European Youth Planning Conference*. Contributions by B.T. Molander, J. Hoekendijk, G.H. Booth, J. Fraser.

Ecumenical Institute, Bossey, 3-8 January 1951: *The Churches' Responsibilities for Children and Young People in Need of Care: Aims and Methods in their Education*. See *Report of the Study Conference on the Churches' Responsibilities*, 1951.

Schmie, Stuttgart, FRG, 24 April-4 May 1951: *European Youth Leaders' Conference*. Two addresses by W.A. Visser 't Hooft.

Ecumenical Institute, Bossey, 26-30 October 1951: *European Christian Youth Editors' Conference*. Contributions by H.H. Brunner, A. Finet, P. Guinness, C. Lund-Quist, J. Ryberg, E. Stammler.

Presinge, Switzerland, 6-9 November 1951: *Fifth European Youth Planning Conference*. Contributions by R. Tobias, B.T. Molander, R. Mackie.

Bonn, FRG, 28-29 February 1952: *Consultation of Representatives of Church Youth Councils in Europe*. The meeting was convened by the Dutch Ecumenical Youth Council.

Haslev, Denmark, 22-29 April 1952: *European Youth Leaders' Training Conference*. Three aims: (1) our problems today as churches and in our youth work; (2) our opportunities today as challenged by secular ideologies; (3) God's possibilities today with our churches and our youth work. Contributions by N. Soe, H. Poelchau, R. de Pury, J. Huxtable.

Berlin, FRG, 1-3 May 1952: *European Youth Leaders' Conference*. Problems and concerns with East-German youth leaders were shared.

Ecumenical Institute, Bossey, 16-19 September 1952: *Sixth European Youth Planning Conference*. European youth giving to be extended to a world basis and preparations for the Travancore World Christian Youth Conference.

Ecumenical Institute, Bossey, 27 April-3 May 1953: *The Place and Function of Youth Work in the Church.* Contributions by H. Kraemer, J. Lochard, E.H. Patey, E. van Bruggen.

Begnins, Switzerland, 13-16 October 1953: *Seventh Consultation of European National Youth Secretaries.* Preparation for youth participation in the Evanston Assembly. Contributions by W.A. Visser 't Hooft, M. Kohnstamm, Père Villain, H.H. Harms.

Berlin, FRG, 26 April-4 May 1954: *European Youth Leaders Conference. Christ, the Hope of the World.* Contributions by A. Nikolainen, D. Jenkins, J. Meyendorff, H. Pfeiffer, P. Ricoeur.

Crêt-Bérard, Switzerland, 1-6 November 1954: *Eighth Consultation of European National Youth Secretaries.* Evanston follow-up in Europe, world Christian youth commission, YMCA centennial and relations with other organizations were discussed.

Beirut, Lebanon, 18-26 April 1955: *Christian Youth Leaders.* See *Consultation of Christian Youth Leaders,* 1955, which contains addresses by B.T. Molander, J. Meyendorff, G. Tomeh, H. McMullen, Z. Shakhashiri, Y. Hanna, E. Beyouth, W.A. Visser 't Hooft, J. Jesudason, and reports on various Orthodox youth movements and churches in Syria, Lebanon, Jordan, Iran, Iraq, Greece, Cyprus, Egypt and Ethiopia.

Berlin, FRG, 28 April-2 May 1955: *Ecumenical Youth Leaders' Conference. The Race Question.* Contributions by H. Kraemer, R. Bilheimer, M. Barot.

Ecumenical Institute, Bossey, 30 April-8 May 1955: *Ecumenical Training Course for Youth Leaders.* Contributions by H. Lilje, E. Chandler, H.H. Harms, R. Mackie, P. Potter, R. Paul, E. Rees, H. Rohrbach, W. Perkins.

Canterbury, England, 25 August-1 September 1955: *Ecumenism and World Confessionalism.* This youth Faith and Order consultation discussed five concerns: (1) the relation of Christ and the church; (2) the nature and problems of ecumenical worship; (3) world confessionalism and ecumenism; (4) Christian lay youth movements and the church; (5) the relation of Faith and Order to other ecumenical concerns.

Oud Poelgeest, Holland, 10-15 October 1955: *Ninth Consultation of European National Youth Secretaries. Integration of Young People into the Life of the Church: the Problem.* Contributions by H.O. Wölber, M. Visser.

Berlin, FRG, 23 April-1 May 1956: *Ecumenical Youth Leaders' Conference. Stand Fast in the Faith.* Contributions by G. Bassarak, J. Meisel, T. Vinay.

Ecumenical Institute, Bossey, 11-16 June 1956: Conference on Education in the Armed Forces. Problems of young people serving in the armed forces were discussed.

Crêt-Bérard, Switzerland, 5-12 October 1956: *Tenth European Ecumenical Youth Secretaries Consultation.* Five concerns: (1) integration of young people in the life of the church; (2) European youth matters; (3) ecumenical work camps; (4) ecumenical youth conference in Europe 1959; (5) ecumenical youth centres, conferences and intervisitation.

Berlin, FRG, 26 April-4 May 1957: *European Youth Leaders Conference. The Christian Community in a Changing World.* Contributions by I. Becker, H.G. Dänel, R. Moussay, H.W. Boersma-Smit.

Hamburg, FRG, 7-12 October 1957: *Eleventh European Ecumenical Youth Secretaries Consultation.* Contributions by K. Bridston, H. Schmidt. Concerns: ecumenical youth work, international Christian youth exchange, relations to Christian world youth bodies.

Hilversum, Holland, 6-11 January 1958: *Baptism and Confirmation.* Contributions by J.K.S. Reid, Principal Dykes, Superintendent Frerichs.

Mitaka, Tokyo, Japan, 2-6 August 1958: *Asian Youth Work.* Sponsored by WCCE, the WCC Youth Department and the EACC.

Crêt-Bérard, Switzerland, 28 October-1 November 1958: *Twelfth European Youth Secretaries Consultation.* General survey of youth matters in Europe.

Sigtuna, Sweden, 15-17 November 1959: *Thirteenth European Youth Secretaries Consultation.* Contributions by A. Booth, H.H. Harms, P. Edwall, O. Engström. Preparations for Lausanne conference.

Driebergen, Holland, 11-15 January 1960: *Holy Communion and Youth.* Contributions by H. Berkhof, K. Grayston, Max Thurian.

Seengen (Aargau) Switzerland, 16-18 October 1960: *Ecumenical Youth Service Consultation.* See *Resolutions on Ecumenical Work Camps,* 1960.

Seengen (Aargau), Switzerland, 18-23 October 1960: *Fourteenth Consultation of European Ecumenical Youth Secretaries.* Contributions by P. Potter, Frère Laurent.

Nyon, Switzerland, 21-24 November 1960: *Leadership.* See *Leadership: Reflections Following a World Christian Youth Commission Consultation,* 1961, which includes contributions by P.M. Limbert, H.-R. Weber, E. Barker, R.N. Mould.

Lincoln, England, 16-20 January 1961: *Youth and Evangelism.* Contributions by N. Beets, W. Killinger, G. Rupp, E. Southcott.

Ecumenical Institute, Bossey, 1-4 March 1961: *Services of Holy Communion at Ecumenical Gatherings.* See *The Ecumenical Review,* Vol. 13, No. 3, April 1961, pp.353-364. The consultation was held under the auspices of the Youth Department and Faith and Order.

Oberbarmen, Radevormwald, FRG, 10-14 October 1961: *Fifteenth Consultation of European Youth Secretaries.* Contributions by A.H. van den Heuvel, P. Löffler, C.I. Itty, A. Brandenburg, C.A. de Ridder, G. Williams.

Torre Pellice, Italy, October 1961: *Youth Assembly.* See *Ecumenical Youth News,* No. 6, September-October 1961. Speakers were R. Beaupère, Bishop Emilianos, W.A. Visser 't Hooft, considering the significance of the New Delhi Assembly, 1961, and the Second Vatican Council.

New Delhi, India, 10-17 November 1961: *Assembly Youth Delegates Meeting.* See *Ecumenical Youth News,* No. 7, November 1961, and No. 1, January 1962. The conference reflected on the concerns of unity, witness and service, the New Delhi Assembly and the future of the WCC Youth Department.

Ecumenical Institute, Bossey, 28 March-1 April 1962: *The Impact of Secondary Education on Young People.* See *The Impact of Secondary Education on Young People and its Implications for the Christian Youth Movements,* Geneva, World Christian Youth Commission, 1962. Contributions by D.E. Woods, P. Wells, H. Makulu, M. Gibbs, E. Adler, J.M. Mitchell, L.P. Fitzgerald, F.J. Glendenning, R. Stöver, J.P. van Praag.

Bièvres, France, 9-13 October 1962: *Sixteenth Consultation of European Ecumenical Youth Secretaries.* Contributions by A.H. van den Heuvel, O. Clément, J. Beaumont, R. Bilheimer, C. Bäumler.

Bièvres, France, October 1962: *The Missionary Structure of the Congregation.* See *Ecumenical Youth News*, No. 7, October 1962. National Roman Catholic Youth organizations in Austria, the Netherlands and Switzerland participated.

Ecumenical Institute, Bossey, 25-30 March 1963: *Bible Reading Notes and Biblical Theology.* See *Report of a Consultation on Bible Reading Notes and Biblical Theology.* Contributions by G. Amsler, G. Galitis, W. Harrelson, P. Jones, C. Maurer, E.H. Robertson, A.G. Smith, W.A. Visser 't Hooft, C.M. de Vries, C.W. Welsh.

Rochester, USA, 17-22 August 1963: *Confessionalism and the Ecumenical Movement.* Papers on world confessional bodies and world confessionalism and ecumenical youth work served as background material.

Geneva, Switzerland, 2-5 October 1963: *World Confessionalism.* This consultation continued the discussion of a meeting at Rochester, USA, 17-22 August 1963.

Josefstal, FRG, 7-11 October 1963: *Seventeenth Consultation of Ecumenical Youth Secretaries in Europe.* Contributions by P. Krusche, P. Dominice, J.H. van Beusekom, A.H. van den Heuvel, R. Schweizer.

Mexico City, Mexico, 8-20 December 1963: *Divided Witness.* See *Ecumenical Youth News*, No. 1, January 1964. Youth delegates participated in the first meeting of the Commission on World Mission and Evangelism.

Broumana, Lebanon, 2-12 July 1964: *Behold, I Make all Things New.* See *Ecumenical Youth News*, No. 6, September 1964. The meeting was part of the "Life and Mission of the Church" study of the WSCF, co-sponsored by the WCC Youth Department.

Zeist, Holland, 9-10 October 1964: *European National Correspondents.* National reports were received and relationships with the CEC and the WCCE explored.

Zeist, Holland, 12-16 October 1964: *Youth in a Complex Society.* See *Youth*, No. 10, November 1964. Contributions by P. Kramer, J.G. Davies, P. Brenac, C.M. Matthey, O. Nisser, K. Bliss, H. Hoefnagels.

Lincoln, England, 19-24 April 1965: *Conversion in a Secular Age.* "Conversion to God and Men", by Paul Löffler, and an extensive bibliography on conversion and secularization served as background papers.

Ecumenical Institute, Bossey, 3-8 May 1965: *Christian Education and Ecumenical Commitment.* See *Risk*, Vol. II, No. 1, pp.1-126. The consultation was organized by the Faith and Order Secretariat, the Youth Department and the WCCE. Contributions by J.K.S. Reid, L. Vischer, G. Downey, E.G. Rupp, D. van der Plas, M.B. Handspiker, R. Henderlite, H. Archibald.

Thessalonica, Greece, 5-11 September 1965: *Youth in the Modern World.* A conference of younger theologians of Eastern and Western traditions. Contributions by G.M. van Asperen, C. Davey, W. Gorzewski, G. Khodr, J. Lambrinidis, N. Nissiotis, B. Rigdon, P. Stolt, E. Voulgarakis, C. Yiannaras.

Koppelsberg, Plön, FRG, 14-15 October 1966: *European National Correspondents*. Relationship between national correspondents and the appeal to the young, European walk, and ecumenical diary in Europe.

Koppelsberg, Plön, FRG, 17-21 October 1966: *International Economic Justice*. Contributions by A.H. van den Heuvel, E.N.E. Udoh, H. de Lange, S. Parmar, R. Padrun.

Annecy, France, 1-6 April 1967: *Unattached Youth*. See *Ecumenical Press Service*, No. 14, 20 April 1967. The Youth Departments of the WCC and the WCCE, the WSCF and the World's YMCA and YWCA sponsored this consultation. Participants gave account of their work among youth in Amsterdam, Berlin, Birmingham, Glasgow, London and Paris. Understood by the term "unattached" were those people whose needs are not met by the usual types of organized activities.

Duisburg, FRG, August 1967: *Revolution: the Struggle for True Humanity*. See *Ecumenical Youth News*, No. 7, September 1967. The conference was sponsored by the International Christian Youth Exchange, the WSCF's secondary schools work programme and the European working group of the WCC Youth Department.

Wiener-Neustadt, Austria, 9-14 October 1967: *European National Correspondents*. Contributions by J. Pronk, A. Abrahamowicz, H.J. Benedict, P. Bouman, J.F.J. Glendenning, B. Gran, G. Khodr, P. Rechman, E.F. Winter.

Geneva, Switzerland, 6-9 February 1968: *World Christian Youth Organizations*. See *Ecumenical Youth News*, No. 2, February 1968. The YMCA, YWCA, WSCF, the World Federation of Catholic Women and Girls, the International Young Catholic Students and other Roman Catholic organizations met to explore closer relationships and cooperation.

Berlin, GDR, 22-26 April 1968: *All European Seminar*. Contributions by P. Potter, T. Christopherson, W. Hollenweger.

Uppsala, Sweden, 1-3 July 1968: *Pre-Assembly Youth Participants' Conference 1968*. See *Ecumenical Youth News*, No. 6, June 1968. The gathering issued a statement declaring that youth is anxious to participate in the Assembly to the fullest possible extent. It accused delegates of being "too old, too wordy, and too ready to compromise".

Cava dei Tirreni, Italy, 11-19 July 1970: *Encounter at Cava*. See: *Encounter at Cava*. Sixth theological encounter between younger theologians of Orthodox, Protestant and Catholic traditions, 1970.

WCC Sub-unit on Youth 1971-

Geneva, Switzerland, 1-4 May 1973: *Black Theology and Latin American Theology of Liberation*. See *Risk*, Vol. 9, No. 2, 1973. Papers were given by J.H. Cone, H. Assmann, P. Freire, E.I. Bodipo-Malumba.

Windsor Castle, England, 8-17 May 1975: *Spirituality Workshop*. See *Risk*, Vol. 12, No. 2, 1976. The workshop concentrated on the worship of the Uppsala Assembly, a consultation on "Worship in a Secular Age" in Geneva in 1969 and the Faith and Order Commission meeting at Louvain in 1971.

Arusha, Tanzania, December 1975: *Pre-Assembly Youth Meeting*.

Ecumenical Institute, Bossey, 10-24 July 1978: *Christian Vigilance and Solidarity on Six Continents.* See *Youth Newsletter*, Vol. 2, No. 1, April 1978. An ecumenical cooperative venture for students, organized by Bossey, the WSCF, PTE and the Youth Office.

Ayia Napa, Cyprus, 13-20 July 1978: *Christian Youth in a Troubled Society.* See *Christian Youth in a Troubled Society*, 1978. See also *Youth Newsletter*, Vol. 2, No. 3, December 1978. Contributions by W. Kheir, Bishop G. Khodr, S. Sahiouny, F. Haddad, Bishop G. Haddad, T. Mitri, P. Moss.

Stony Point, USA, 6-8 September 1978: *International Dimensions of Youth and Young Adult Ministries.* See *Youth Newsletter*, Vol. 2, No. 2, summer 1978. Sponsored by Canadian and US denominations in ministries with youth in conjunction with the Sub-unit on Youth.

Wellesley, Massachusetts, 6-11 July 1979: *Faith, Science and the Future.* See *Youth Newsletter*, Vol. 3, No. 2, June 1979 and Vol. 3, No. 3, September 1979. A pre-conference to the world conference on "Faith, Science and the Future" in Boston, USA, 12-24 July 1979.

Leningrad, USSR, 28 March-5 April 1981: *Regional Youth Secretaries.* See *Youth Working Group — Regional Youth Secretaries Meeting, 1981.* Regional reports were given by F. Oshige (Latin America), I. Cambridge (Caribbean), G. Hickel (Europe), R. Jarjour (Middle East), C. Magiga (Africa). Other reports were given on: stewards programme, world youth projects, ecumenical youth service, faith and justice course, Sixth Assembly and pre-Assembly youth event and preparations.

Vancouver, Canada, 17-21 July 1983: *Pre-Assembly Youth Event.* See *Youth Newsletter*, Vol. 7, No. 3, September 1983. A message to the WCC Sixth Assembly was issued.

Appendix III: Executive Secretaries of the WCC Youth Department

Jean M. Fraser	1947-1954
Bengt-Thure Molander	1954-1957
Philip A. Potter	1957-1960
Roderick French	1960-1964
Albert H. van den Heuvel	1964-1968
William J. Nottingham	1968
Oscar Bolioli	1968-1972
Archibald Le Mone	1972-1975
Robert Welsh	1976
Peter Moss	1976-1982
Carlos A. Sintado	1982-1985
Heikki Huttunen	1986-